THE PANHANDLE PIRATES

CONNOR FLYNN

BEYOND THE FRAY

Publishing

ISBN 13: 978-1-954528-37-6

Cover design: Disgruntled Dystopian Publications

Beyond The Fray Publishing, a division of Beyond The Fray, LLC, San
Diego, CA
www.beyondthefraypublishing.com

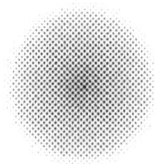

BEYOND THE FRAY

Publishing

CONTENTS

CHAPTER 1
LAUNCH

Haunted funeral home. Calhoun County, Florida.

This world is full of uncertainties and insecurities but I feel at ease when searching for answers with my people. Teamwork makes the dream work, remember that when it's pouring. I'm Connor the Countryman and I ride with my crew like Harry Potter on this magical journey. We meander through the muggle illusion while the Sun's up and dive deep into the mysterious underworld of our reality in the moonlight. We wax on, wax off with Mr. Miyagi in the hidden realm and this is my journal documenting our adventures. You never know what to expect when we all get together, so raise your sights and be ready for some frights. The vibes are rare, be there for a scare! Yo ho ho!

Freddie Kruger mural. Jackson County, Florida.

After living near Buccaneer Bay and visiting Jean Lafitte's stash spots, I found myself gravitating towards lost treasure and fallen relics almost every single day. I fell back into the days of rewatching Hook over and over, pretending to be a Lost Boy battling gators and crooks. I always had a knack for sniffing out the bs from the real. As the son of a twin, my antennas were made for a reason and I plan on putting the power to good use. And as a descendent of Bootstrap Bill Turner and William Junior, I plan on finding loot like the Goonies and hopefully something even deeper like Sam and Jared from the Zephyr mission. It's all about the journey, we need to live in the moment but try to feel these with me coz dead men tell no tales.

I have written about my Mohican adventures with Adam, surviving Tennessee with Jake, and fleeing the wolfman with Alex back at Sleepy Hollow. I've told you about my childhood on the farm and overnight stays at the firehouse. You've heard about my run-ins with the Ohio Grassman, Crybaby Bridges, and the Witches Ball but this is something new, something strange... The stars have guided me down the buckeye boulevard to the swamp for a reason and I think I may have a lead on it. Follow me off plank, things are gonna get dank.

I have been searching for two things ever since I moved near the Garden of Eden and that is, treasure and answers. I'm searching for the bridge to our creator. I have located the map but sadly the monsters stand in my way. I have gone deep into Davy Jones locker and compiled a gang of misfits to aid me on my adventures. We are the Panhandle Pirates and this is our storm. All hand hoy, ahoy me hearties!

I met Sabre during my first week at the shop but it

felt like we have known one another from somewhere long before. He got the nickname Sabrecat coz he was always finding something prehistoric. A true sea dog. We immediately clicked. He was interested in scary movies, knew all about fishing, and was a military veteran... so he had my respect. It didn't take long for me to open up about ghosts and bigfoot with him. I wasn't very surprised when he told me that he had multiple strange encounters over the years. He even said he had a giant bone!

Abandoned Monticello church. Jackson County, Florida.

We bonded over our cryptid experiences and love for superheroes but also on a deeper level. We are both outcasts and take true pride in that. I enjoy walking my walk on the fringe of society and so does Sabre. The world is a very strange place and most people want to wear a blindfold, we are not part of that herd. We chase that pot of gold even if it means they make fun of us for believing in leprechauns. I grew with the luck of the Irish in my blood...I know magic is real and I'm not alone.

These two brothers started showing up at my shop pretty frequently. They were really into Magic the Gathering and abstract 360 games. It didn't take long til we were talking about cryptids and theories. They mentioned they had a family legend of a creature on their property, the hog-nosed bear. The guys had my attention! They explained it with conviction and invited me out to investigate. These scalawags were true buckaroos and I saw Blackbeard potential in em!

The fellas had a plethora of knowledge and outdoor skills. They also had multiple encounters with gremlins, fairies, and Bigfoot himself. They had a great eye for tracks and fossils. The guys proved to be valuable team members in just the first few adventures and have been a staple along the journey ever since. That's Tristin and Cam and they represent Hidden Relief! They became brothers and are now mine...

We all have been judged, harassed, stalked and even hunted but continue to push forward. Our glasses might fog up but we trust our steps. We laugh at their threats.. We are one with our instincts and believe that our experience will lead to insight. We come prepared for anything and everything but ultimately seek answers with the deepest respect. We work hard to walk this path. It is not easy but we have been molded for this purpose. We will overcome the speed bumps the watchers have placed in our path.

Sabre is part Native American. He also spent years overseas and gained ancient knowledge from the locals. His diverse training brings a plethora of vibrations and angles to our adventures. His awareness and sixth sense mixed with my background of cross country couchsurfing and off grid urban exploring creates an asterisk. The brothers bring an interesting duality to the table. Twins are powerful but a transformer is a catalyst. The product of our frequencies attract many unique anomalies on our journey. We were meant to make this mission. It was written in stone.

Ninjacat lived in Washington State at the foothills of Mt. Rainer for some time. He has heard his share of stories of cryptid reports and missing people. It is one of the most dangerous volcanoes in the world. It is covered in tons of glacial ice and it would cause major floods if it erupted. The ninja has always been a prospector and a fossil hunter. It is interesting that his path of life has brought him to many hot spot locations for oddities and abnormalities.

Sabre was stationed at Fort Lewis Washington and often heard of the "big animals" nearby. The military base has a long history of sasquatch encounters and strange sightings. One soldier even shot one of the creatures in the seventies... There are still occurrences being reported and leaking out almost every week! Cat Lake, Theander Lake, and Elk Plain are all hotspots in Pierce County. JBLM is one of many military bases with high action with these creatures, it raises the questions, what are they truly after?

The ninja spent time at haunted Fort Benning in Columbus, Georgia as well. Many soldiers have reported strange experiences while spending time on the grounds. There is an entity that looks like Samara from The Ring that has been spotted creeping around camp. Fallen comrades are said to still roam the region as well. The historic town is famous for many phantoms and spectres. Captain also trained at Fort Hood, which has an entire different spider web of problems down in Texas! The chupacabra and wood boogers are the least of their worries!

I grew up on Lake Erie and spent a lot of my childhood exploring the unknown. The road took me across the states and back down to the swamp. Living out of my car and on the outskirts of reality has taught me many things. It has guided me on a path of enlightenment and hardship. I have become tough like a rock but I'm ready to roll like marble. I just hope I land softly... We are all just protons and electrons. We spend most time in particle form but I am pursuing the answers of the wave. How is our DNA older than Earth itself? Where are we from?

I've investigated creatures in the Honey Island Swamp, Great Lakes and deep in the mountains. I've researched true crime, missing people, and unexplained phenomena my entire life. I have always been interested in folklore and journalism. The Witches Ball and Crybaby Bridge were a big part of my childhood so it is no surprise they still lurk my dreams. I am in a constant pursuit of truth and expansion of consciousness. There is so much history in this world and I am just attempting to tap into some of the streams. I am trying to access hidden realms.

By the end of this collection, you might understand how we ended up where we have. You might see a gleam of how we drew our conclusions. You will need to find the connections that we traced in the stars. They were illustrated long ago.. You may have to read between the lines. We have left a trail of breadcrumbs. The dark truth is, you might have to finish our story. You might have to write the final chapter. You might have to put together the tablets and draw your own conclusions. Close your eyes, you already have the answers.

We are diving into some deep holes that might not have a way out. We are climbing some walls that we might not be able to cross back over. We are going back in time to see when our life lines first intertwined. Energy was never created nor destroyed. It has always existed. The red string on our ankle was tied long before this lifetime. Coincidence is the only thing to never exist. We need to begin to think and live untraditionally. We have to break free from the binds that control us. The only chance we have at clarity, is inward. Pay attention to your dreams, be weary of your thoughts. Don't spell words that you don't

Remember that safety is our priority. Our plan is to have more plans. People are vanishing in mysterious numbers while hiking and hunting so we keep our heads on a swivel. We pack extra supplies and always tell someone where we are going. We have heard stories from across the world but just as many tales from our own hood. Mysteries are just around the corner so please lock your door. If there is a storm coming, please get home.

Our voyage will cross haunted bridges and dive deep into red rock canyons. We will fish brackish water, visit American pyramids, and stay overnight within haunted walls. We will be searching for signs of strange creatures and our ancestors' lost belongings. In our investigation, we will turn campfire stories into real life legends. Who built the ziggurats? Who carved the bayous? Are they trying to rebuild the Tower of Babel? Why did they fake the space launch? And what the heck are they hiding below the Gulf of Mexico?

Through exploration, meditation, and experimentation we hope to receive the answers we are looking for.

When was the red thread tied around our ankles? And who is the architect? Let's find out! Join the Panhandle Pirates and you might find some treasure! Beware of the cryptids, coz nothing comes easy! The kraken is waiting, the kraken is the gate. The clap of thunder sparks the first burp.

CHAPTER 2
THE GHOST OF BELLAMY BRIDGE

Bellamy Bridge after Midnight

The story of Elizabeth Bellamy and the haunted bridge sends chills up the spines of almost everybody in the Panhandle. The tragic events on her wedding day led to an eternal flame being lit deep in the Florida swamps. Nocturnal tourists and satanists alike both visit the rusty structure for the rare energy. Orbs and strange sounds have been captured along the trail and we have had a few of our own that literally left a mark.

According to legend, Elizabeth Bellamy died on her wedding day and still roams the regional swamps. Her wedding dress caught on fire and she dove into the water head first. She died a painful death and promised her husband that she would forever be with him. Historians claim the true story is that Elizabeth and her daughter died of malaria and the husband killed himself at the Chattahoochee Landing after suffering from a broken heart. No matter the origin, the story is truly heartbreaking.

Locals have captured strange mist and flashes in photographs. Aerial phenomenon and piercing animal sounds seem to always be present for visitors. There is a blanket of unique energy that sweeps the forest when the sun goes down. I've heard stories of people being greeted by a ghostly horse and carriage while others just heard it from a distance. The mind will play tricks on you in the swamp. Be careful!

Our very first adventure together was at Bellamy Bridge. We planned it for a while with our buddy Dom from the smoke shop. He was ex military as well and hiked all across the dense terrain of Hawaii. He lived in

Tallahassee so we were a little bound for time but one night it finally lined up.

The weather was crappy and I was tired from working all day but the window was open! I packed some water and grabbed a flashlight from the store. We rode out and headed towards the haunted bridge. We passed by Sunland and I mentioned the anomalies there. There have been many reports of screams and shadows in the night. It was an old Air Force Base and was home to the Smiley Face serial killer. He has since died…

We pulled up to the trail and I was so excited. The storm had ravaged the area but I was still optimistic about finding the structure. We followed the dirt path for a quarter mile and then the fallen trees became too much. We circled around them and began getting off track. The sun was going down and it had just started drizzling. The canopy covered a lot of the rain but the moisture in the air created a humid chamber that we were now trapped in. We had to climb over or crawl under huge logs every couple steps.

We continued on this treacherous path for a good forty minutes and it felt like we were going in circles. We were all exhausted and starting to grow more and more frustrated. We finally checked the GP on our phones and we were in the middle of the forest! We looked up to the skies to help with navigation and seemed to be put into a trance. There were two moons. We couldn't figure out the illusion. We twisted and turned around with the electric compass but it was playing games in our mind. Our only choice was to push forward and hopefully find the river.

My glasses were fogging up and I was starting to get a bit worried. I was not prepared to spend the night out here. My jacket was soaked and I was burning up, sweating underneath. We started hearing sounds within a hundred yards. There were footfalls on twigs sticks plus strange bird calls from time to time. We also saw some hog tracks and just felt a strange feeling in the air.

Cassie holding Cabbage Man Cast near Chipola River

I was worried about stepping on a snake or twisting my ankle. We had no clue which direction to the parking lot and this had to be the third time we stepped through this creek bed. We kept running into flooded sections of the swamp. We heard movement in the shallow water but I wanted no part of that. We finally made it to a clearing and found this washed up walkway. I would later find out that we were pretty close to the iron bridge at that moment.

Instead we got sidetracked and went in the wrong direction. The thicket was getting worse and so was our condition. The flashlight began to flash and then suddenly went out. Now we just had our phones… We were screwed! We gave up on the river and I began leading the way. Just b-lining it toward the direction we believed the road to be. I looked back toward the guys and fell down a bank.

I got up and stumbled to my feet. I was shifted into another realm. I fumbled forward and saw the river gleaming below the moon. I could hear the structure rattling in the wind and heard a big noise in the water. A white aura emerged from the surface and floated towards me. That was Elizabeth Bellamy. I was not threatened. I felt like she was there to guide me. She flew into me and I woke up.

The guys were laughing at me and coming to pick me up. I was back on two legs with a new pep in my step. I knew we were going in the right direction but there would still be obstacles on other paths. I barged forward and the guys followed behind. I was blinded by the fog on my goggles but the frequencies were calling my name.

We heard cars on the road and knew we were getting close. We kept moving and heard some car doors slam. We ducked down and remained quiet. I wasn't trying to explain my ghost hunting passion to the police. And I was definitely not prepared to battle some satanists. They took off down one path and we squeezed back into the parking lot.

We got out of there quickly and rode towards my store. We grabbed gatorade and burned one in the car. We reminisced on a wild night. We wondered about electromagnetic interference and lunar anomalies. We laughed about it being a good start to a special bond of adventuring.

On the way home, Dom almost got car jacked. Sabre almost hit a deer and I got pulled over. I was shivering and still soaking wet. On the last turn before my street, I crossed over the yellow line a bit to avoid some hurricane debris. They thought I was drunk and rang the lights. I was honest and told them I was dehydrated and just popped a tire the week before. Luckily they understood and gave me a pass. I have to thank Mrs. Bellamy for that one…

We have returned to the bridge on multiple occasions. One night I recorded a whoop after being out there for a couple hours. Not long after, a tree went crashing down. I took that as a warning. Another night, something jumped off into the swamp when we approached it. Badly flooded now but I can't wait to visit one day by kayak. Now that would be a spooky site to roll up on! This spot in the swamp is definitely one of my favorites...

CHAPTER 3
ALAMO CAVE OF HINSON'S CONSERVATION
HIGHWAY 73, FL

Entrance to cave.

The conservation is a little known oasis not far from downtown Marianna. Down the bumpy hill, there is a plethora of fossils, caves, and even a cabin tucked within the grounds. Native Americans and ancient animals called Hinson's home in the olden days but now the panthers and boar reside in the woods. The Chipola winds through and brings a lot of visitors, now let's see who has the Eagle Eye and can find the Alamo!

Highway 73 is home to many mysteries. Donnie Miller from Standing Goats Rescue had a close encounter with a sasquatch while clearing hogs out of a farm. One plantation is on the cover of ZombiEarth and Tristin heard a story of a sinkhole with a green eyed monster in the bottom. So beware when you are near the Iron Bridge or under the concrete one!

We pulled down the rocky road and past the old railroad. I was smiling from ear to ear. After the hurricane, the park was closed for a good while and I thought I never would have had the chance to visit. Now the gate was back open and I was ready for the voyage! We parked our car and set off on a strange angle away from the path.

Sabercat said he knew a quicker way of finding the cave and had a couple other spots that he wanted to show me. We trekked through the tall grass and watched out for rattlesnakes. I was worried about ticks, they love tall weeds. We made it to a path and it was beautiful. There were tall walls of rock that were full of fossils. We took our time digging in them.

Checking out history.

We continued down the path and found an abandoned cabin! We didn't bother going in but it was really cool. I would have loved to spend the night there for a couple nights. I would surely be on high alert. Pretty far from humanity and who knows what lives below the caves! Just the threat of panther and bear would make taking out the trash a little spooky.

We were getting close to the cave and I could feel it. I remember watching the Florida Trailblazer adventuring down here. I still couldn't get over the feeling of after the hurricane when I thought I was robbed of the chance to soak in the essence of shelters. That horror evaporated when we approached the hole in the wall! I peeked down for monsters and almost rolled in!

I was in heaven. I had found the Alamo! I remember reading about the Native American artifacts and extinct animal bones that were discovered here. Dale Cox said most of the arrowheads were made while they were in the hole under attack. I tried to investigate every inch of the walls and floor looking for carvings or any other remnants of the past. You could feel the ancient presence in the air. Animals and men alike have taken shelter down here. Fires have been burned and lessons have been learned.

We soaked in the vibes until it was time for the next adventure. Captain mentioned another cave nearby. He said he recently visited and heard strange children's voices. My eyes widened and we were back on the trail. We came to a thick creek that we needed to cross. We marched up and down looking for a skinny part to cross. We began gathering supplies to build a bridge. That plan fell through quickly when we realized how deep the creek was…

We adventured some more and looked for hidden treasure. We searched for the Cabin Fever geocache but had no luck. I'm not sure if we were off on our coordinates or it was destroyed by the storm. Hopefully it is replanted and we can put some gems in the case to trade. Love signing the log in sheets with something about bigfoot.

Rock stacks of Alamo.

There were other ancient civilizations in the area. This park was holy land. There are some huge sinkholes in the area. The most famous caves alongside the Chipola River are called the Ovens. I wasn't able to get my eyes on them on this adventure but I definitely plan on kayaking the area and checking it out. I have watched a handful of videos online about them and that's one of my next bucket list.

I imagined the railroad cutting through here in the olden days. It surely had to be breathtaking with the crystal blue water and luscious forests. I'm sure they saw a ton of wildlife. There are a ton of pecan trees and wildflowers! The remnants of the forgotten railway definitely add a historic vibe to the hidden oasis. They probably had no idea of all the deep caves full of artifacts in the region...

We made it back to the truck and there were a couple cars parked on the road up ahead. They stopped at a puddle that we maneuvered around. It was a little suspicious but I'm pretty sure they were city workers. They were just sitting in their cars on the phone. We rolled past them and waved! Definitely a legendary first trip to the Alamo!

I'm typing this sunburnt as hell. The day before the solar eclipse we returned back to Hinson's. I kayaked all morning with Tristin and then joined with the ninja down under. We hiked Alamo and then crossed the creek to do more exploring. We found some cool stones and T found an opening. It was a yellow jacket cave, the place Captain sat on a nest and got stung over fifty times. Luckily no bees this time but we still made a buzz!

We returned for Tristin's birthday. We soaked in the vibes before we saw Shyamalan's OLD at the cinema. He said he heard a clapping sound coming from the woods to our right. It could have been a bird or it may have been the troll trying to lure us. We stuck to the path and hung out in the cave. There was a huge splash in the water after a while of chillin'. Now that was chilling! Few weeks later, I returned with Donnie Miller and then Jack McClellan. This place attracts all sorts of legends!

CHAPTER 4
GOPHERWOOD AND THE GARDEN OF EDEN
BRISTOL, FL

The Overlook. Bristol, Florida

T he Garden of Eden trail is sacred soil. The region is unlike any other in the sunshine state. The deep valleys and diverse wildlife provide the perfect oasis for all visitors. The park holds twenty-seven of the twenty-eight trees mentioned in the Bible. The river delta also breaks into four rivers like the good book describes. There are only two places like that in the known world. This place is truly special.

I just released Erie Swamps Roadtrip to Eden and wanted to see Ground Zero as a new man. I showed Captain some videos about the trail history and a few Alum Bluff fossil voyages. We packed our bags and were ready to go. I told him to prepare for the most strenuous hike in the state. He took my advice but there is no way to truly prepare for a journey through the seventh Heaven.

On the road, I pointed out the Corner Bar that had been destroyed by the storm. I told that our buddy, Dylan, and his grandparents built that place and I regretted never stopping by. After umpiring, I would always tell myself next time but when the hurricane struck, I ran out of opportunities. I showed him a couple more cool spots along the way. He loved the story of the Woman in the Swamp along Route 20. We looked for her but had no luck.

As we crossed the time zone, I told him a little archaic knowledge about the path we would be investigating. Twenty-seven of the twenty-eight trees mentioned in the Bible reside in this park. The delta that breaks into four rivers that occurs here is described in the good book as well. The only other place is Siberia. And my favorite fun fact was that torreya is also known as gopherwood. The same stuff Noah used to build the Ark. The only place it grows is right here in these woods. This was truly a sacred place.

After we knew it, we were pulling up to the parking lot and my heart was racing. I was ready to explore ancient history but also nervous about what else is out there. Last time I hiked these paths, I was stranded on a cliffside and stalked by something big. The adventure before that, I came face to face with a giant Eastern diamondback snake. The true serpent of Eden. Rainstorms and sketchy transients are also big risks. But when Arcadia calls, you answer.

I picked up a pamphlet and hit the trail. We passed the water tank and our journey began. We were in the desert phase and would soon be in some dense forests. I read through the paper and told him that we would pass a tornado location and some Civil War battlegrounds. I warned him of venomous critters but also the giant log sized serpents in the wetlands too. We laughed and kept our eyes peeled.

After a while we heard music from deeper in the woods. It was puzzling but we got our answer pretty quickly. We noticed four pretty girls marching above us with a little puppy. They were trekking. We climbed up and met at the crease in the path. We exchanged hellos and asked them if they saw anything cool. They mentioned a big turtle and some squirrels. We pet the dog and wished them well. I debated on telling them about my sasquatch page but ultimately left them in peace. Cool places bring cool people.

Pirates in action. L-R (Tristin, Cam, Connor)

We continued on the path and noticed some deer tracks. The birds were chirping and following us to the river. We took our time because the valleys and steep inclines were tough on our backs and knees. I carried the backpack and water for us. I've learned over my experiences in Eden to pace myself. Migraines creep up quickly and delirium will approach abruptly, leaving us vulnerable.

We finally made it to the overlook. We explored the edge and took some photos. I made a video talking about my book and the history of the place. I sat on the bench and opened up our lunch. I embraced the sunshine and enjoyed every bite. I washed it down with Gatorade and sparked a blunt. I channeled the ancient people that stood in this same spot observing the tree tops across the way.

I went into detail about Stacy Brown's bigfoot encounter down the river. I told him that they captured the best thermal sasquatch footage ever taken by a civilian. The Brown's have encountered multiple strange creatures in the area. I also mentioned the Bridge's family. That opened the door to werewolves, portals, and many other things that dive deep into quantum physics. The ley lines converge here and the aquifer below holds some secrets.

I snapped back to reality when we heard a loud smack come from down below. It was across the river but not far from the coast line. I thought it was a rock smack but Captain said it sounded like a club against a tree. We moved down the trail a bit and tried to listen below. We sat there for a while as the bird noises faded away and the region fell silent. This might have been the same creature that was watching Adam and I on the cliffside.

I showed Sabre where we got stranded and then followed the river loop. The edges were steep and my legs were getting shaky but I felt much better than last time that my shoes were on this sand. The sun was setting and I knew it would be dark soon. We didn't have any lights and I knew it would be tough to climb some of them incline blindly. I knew we had to pick up the pace.

The great serpent.

We hustled through the trails and washed up at the creek. As we caught our breath, we heard something big rustling in the bushes above. It was about fifteen yards to the right of the track where we had to scale. We were extremely vulnerable and a fall backwards could be fatal. We crossed our fingers that it wasn't a predator and would just leave us alone. I ascended and braced for impact but luckily it kept going in it's direction.

We were out of the valley and back into the desert sand. It felt good to be out of the canopy but we were not in the clear yet. We passed by a controlled burn area and noticed some movement up ahead. It was small but rapid. I was not trying to risk an encounter with a baby rattlesnake so I proceeded with caution. Captain moved some bark with a branch and jumped back. It was a tarantula. We laughed and made it back to the car.

We guzzled down some more Gatorade and I finished my peanut butter crackers. It always feels good to make it back to safety. I peered back down the trail and envisioned the darkness swallowing it up. That place transforms at night and we made it out right before that match was struck. We coasted back home and felt a little closer to Adam and Eve from there on out. Now I see why Noah used the gopherwood from our region!

This May, I was hiking with Tristin and Camo from Hidden Relief at the sacred garden. We got off to a late start and I made sure to text BigCat just so someone knew where we were. During the hike, Tristin found a sasquatch bedding area. It was truly amazing. We looked for scat and animal bones but it was clean. We meditated next to a torreya tree and heard some noises all around us. We kept our eyes closed and remained entranced. The pixies knew we meant them no harm.

When we finished the loop, we ran into the ninja. We hung out for a couple hours until it got really dark and we had quite the voyage back. We heard many strange sounds and the night really came alive. The ancient gopherwood brings the vibes. Multiple people found sky fish and faeries in the footage that we recorded. That place is full of magic...

CHAPTER 5
SEARCHING FOR THE COBRAGATOR OF MERRITT MILL POND

JACKSON COUNTY, FL

Abandoned barracks.

The Mill Pond is known for their crystal clear water, deep diving caves and world record shell cracker fish. Andrew Jackson and his troops visited the blue spring but they were not the first.

Ancient artifacts and prehistoric tools have been found on the grounds and many of their spirits are said to still wander the region. Sharkansas Women's Prison Massacre and Cobragator were both filmed at the pond and I believe there is some truth to their stories!

We were setting up to launch at the boat ramp when a swimmer came down and a boater pulled up. We talked about the fishing and history of the pond. I showed them the movie case and we had a good laugh. The swimmer says there are some huge creatures in that water and the boater paramedic agrees. He told us a story about how they had to save a girl from quick sand just past the landing. He said to be careful in the mud. It swallows you up.

We hopped on the yaks and went paddling. The sun was shining, the water was crystal clear and things couldn't have been better. There were tons of turtles on logs and the mozzies were not too bad. There was barely any traffic on the water. I dipped my hand in the water and reminded myself that this was one of the major reasons for moving south in the first place.

I recorded some incredible go pro footage. I captured birds flying, fish swimming, and even Sabre saving a snapping turtle from being stuck in a tree limb. We stayed close to the bank and kept our eyes out for action. We waved to the people on their porches and navigated between ruins of docks and pointy trees. I'd love to have property on the waterfront here. It truly is paradise. I could feed the fish right here.

We passed Edd Sorrenson's dive shop and talked about his accolades. He is known as one of the most famous cave drivers in the world. He has been involved in some high profile cases. He saved the British diver assisting in the rescue of the soccer team in Tennessee. He successfully recovered bodies in the Dominican Republic. He also saved a young girl in a miracle case where she miraculously found an air pocket and was able to remain calm. Edd also searched for Ben McDaniel in Vortex Springs. That case is still unsolved. Edd is a good man.

We crossed the pond and pulled up to this big rock overhang. We climbed onto the bank and began to explore. I sparked a spliff and started looking for animal tracks and relics. We crawled up the steep hill and found a bunch of recently cleared trees. We ran straight to the roots and looked for arrowheads. No great points but we found a bunch of flint clippings. We were holding ancient history!

We split up for a bit and kept looking around. I heard voices from below on a boat. I was hoping it wasn't the wildlife commission. I'm sure we weren't supposed to be climbing on the bank, let alone adventuring through cleared land. I ducked and dodged between the trees and tried to keep an eye on our kayaks. I didn't want our crap being stolen either!

I looked around for Sabre but couldn't find him. I tried not to panic but I was caught in the middle of many emotions. I was thinking about the law, our belongings and our safety. Missing 411 protocol tells us to stay together. I know it wasn't too rough of terrain but anything can happen. There was definitely a convergence of energy up here so we had to be careful. I kept exploring and luckily the ninja rolled up. He found a sinkhole.

I told him about the voices but we kept exploring. They would have had quite the climb to reach us. That brought us some time. We found a couple more cool pieces of flint and small fossils. After a while, we ran into a hunting blind. We didn't want to get shot or captured on trail cam so we circled back. We found our starting pile and trekked down the hill. I hid behind the rock and peeked for intruders but it seems they finally left us alone. I took a couple pics and climbed back into the yak.

We kept on that bank until we came upon some sunken treasure! There was a classic car that had been rolled down the steep cliffside. It was caught by the trees, half submerged in the mud. Cat said it was stripped so it must have been stolen. He eyed up a couple pieces that he could use for primitive tools. I recorded a video and got a cool shot of a giant spider but the file ended up being corrupted. Very strange, maybe electromagnetic interference.

I ended up getting the footage back and I'm thankful

we did. It was awesome capturing the footage of the car but in the background we may have spotted the elusive skunk ape. Mike from Long Island Bigfoot spotted a dark faced creature watching us from behind a tree over there. It truly shows how close these creatures can silently creep up on us.

A couple more turtles dove in off of their logs as we circled the outside of the pond. Ron taught me the difference between a snakebird and a cormorant, as a pair perched above. They were drying their leaves coz they aren't waterproof. The ninja knew a dope spot to adventure near the recreational part of the pond. He said there was a cave and some ruins of an old restaurant. The urban exploration inside of me exploded as I kept busy with my oars. I absorbed the sunlight with a smile on my face.

We floated above some of the famous diving caves and I imagined the creatures lurking below. My imagination dove into the caves and followed them into middle earth. It led to the land of dragons and draconian masters. The inward sun powers all above. The subterranean chambers of the planet hold all the secrets. The gnomes, trolls, and crawlers are all protecting something. The magnet pulls many creatures.

I snapped back to reality and hurried out of the monster's range. I'll be back to visit the corners of Earth. I'm looking for a dry entrance until I pass my diving course! We continued bobbing and weaving between the cypress trees. We heard some movement up in the bush above us but couldn't get a visual. We kept along the bank until we ran out of real estate. The sound eventually dissipated as we crossed back over the spring.

Cobragator

Ninja pointed toward an island and we headed right for it. The place looked familiar. I had seen it many times on the internet and just had talked about it to my friend the day before with my friend Jessie. It is crazy how everything is connected! The place was fresh in my mind and naturally I was pulled toward the sacred land.

We sat over the dive cave for a while and imagined how deep it went. He pointed up toward the rock face and said there's a cave up there. We parked the kayaks and got onto the bank. As I grabbed my camera, I knocked his boat in the water and then had to retrieve it. I fell in during the process but luckily didn't tip my yak. It took a while and I made it back. I threw my stuff to Sabre and leaped to land.

We got up the rock face and were looking at some carvings from the 1800s. I was taking some pictures and saw an opening in the boulder. I yelled "cave" and took off toward it. I pulled out my flashlight and made sure no serpents or fairies were guarding the entrance. It seemed the coast was clear so I ducked in.

The vibes were spectacular! You could just feel the history seeping in this place. I imagined the natives sitting around their fires. You could see the marks on the ceiling. I looked at Sabre and he was in amazement. This was his spot and he had never been in this cave. He knew of a different one but this was all he knew. I explored all that I could safely get too. I kept my eyes peeled for rattlesnakes. This would be the perfect place for a den.

It looked like some chambers extended on further but I was not prepared to investigate more. I definitely will be back with the proper gear, not soaked in swim wear! We channeled the ancient vibrations and tried to place ourselves in their stream of knowledge. If it were to rain, we would have no problem surviving in the cave. I have definitely been stranded in far worse places.

We climbed out of the cave and tried to circle back around to the ninja's next spot. We climbed up this steep rock wall and leaped across a freaking gallow! We made our own path up top and it felt like Bellamy Bridge all over again. We tried to keep to the old trail but kept having to go around the fallen bush. We ended up in the middle of nowhere and had no choice but to turn back the way we came.

We climbed back down the sketchy place and I had a little bit of a crappy attitude up there. I didn't have much faith in fighting the jungle when we could have just climbed a different steep rock face and at least knew where we were going. We retraced our steps and made it back up the other peak. We searched for the other cave but had trouble finding it coz of the hurricane damage and overgrowth. Shinobi signaled for me to follow him so that's what I did.

We made our way to the ruins and I was mind blown. The place was hauntingly beautiful. The ceiling was collapsing and there was graffiti in every direction but it felt peaceful. I admired the fireplace and attachment building on the side. I blinked and fell back into the golden age of this place. I'm sure business was banging along the crystal blue waters. Wow. How magical?

There was a small landfill and dirt cul-de-sac so we looked for some lost treasure. The place was marked up by deer and raccoons. I kept my eyes peeled for a bigfoot track or anything else strange. Kept my eyes peeled for homeless and feral people. This would have been a perfect place for them to post up with minimal interference. We started walking towards another building but stopped when we noticed electricity. We had to remain incognito.

We snuck back to the restaurant and enjoyed a couple more minutes of peace. It was getting late and we still wanted to find that second cave. The ferns and vines have taken over and it was nearly impossible. We fought through the thicket and may have found the area but just couldn't get down to the small cave hole. We climbed over to the rock cliff and enjoyed the magical view about fifty feet above the springs. I'm sure many chiefs stood in the same exact place.

The den.

We climbed down to our boats and were back off toward the landing. The sun was going down and the temperature was dropping. I was still wet and my body was beginning to slow down. I felt a sting on my leg and noticed an orange spider. I put him on my oar and then he disappeared. I tried to rescue him. He must have climbed in the boat when we were in the cave. It itches badly and started to swell but I was okay. It actually warmed me up a little bit and put me in a little bit of poisonous trance.

We watched woodpeckers and a school of shell crackers swim by. At one point we noticed a huge wake just ahead of us in a lagoon. It had to be a giant snapping turtle or a passing gator. Either way we proceeded with caution but the fear sank with the ripples as we passed. The most dangerous thing is the wasps. There are stumps with nests bigger than basketballs. Chilling to cruise past. Hidden Relief Tristin learned the hard way from an orange sized nest. Ouch!

We crossed the pond one last time to check out this blue barrel that was lodged between trees. We figured it was probably part of someone's dock at one point. I joked that it might have been filled with some substance that mutated all the fish in the pond. Maybe that will be the intro scene to the Cobragator sequel!

We crossed the mental markers that I had set. We pulled up to the abandoned mansion with the awesome dock that is falling to ruins. The gazebo called to me. I wish I could have spent one evening in its hay day. Would have loved to smoke a cigar and sip some whiskey while listening to the wildlife churn. We loaded our boats and I said goodbye to the water for now.

He dropped me off at my car and we made plans to meet up a bit. I stopped by the store and picked up a few things for my mom. I stopped at her house but it was quick because I was still soaked. I went home, showered, and ripped a dab. I chilled out for a while and then heard a knock on the door. It was Sabre. We ordered Mexican Food and watched Miller catch mudcrabs!

As we left to scoop the food, we saw a cute white kitty scouring near my trash. I left her a little food but made a note in my head to grab some at the dollar store. We picked up both foods and found another cat near the house on the way back. I fed them before we devoured dinner. We watched Hawking Lithics for a few hours and were drained!

That night I had an intense dream of being an animal in the forest. I experienced night, day, and all four seasons. I was hungry with a thirst that I just couldn't quench. I was running for what felt like miles. The air started to become fresh as I breathed it in. I closed my eyes, intoxicated and saw the beautiful spring when they opened. A true feast for the vision.

The next day I went out to eat and ran into Jessie's husband, Jason. I told him I just checked out the Shangri-la spot and he brought up the restaurant above. I told him we could definitely camp there but would still probably need a tent. He asked if we found the cave and I shook my head.

Jason said they used to go to the cave when they were boys and had to be lowered down into it. I realized he was talking about the one we didn't find. I told him that we found the other. He continued and said that they found a skill and huge femur bone there years ago. They contacted authorities and they excavated the cave. They said the remains were hundreds of years old. Again, the spider web of connection! We will find that cave!

Returned to the spring for more investigations with Tristin. It was his first time kayaking. He did great. We made it to the caves and restaurant ruins. He cut his foot real bad but was a trooper about it. On the way back, we dodged a large serpent but couldn't get the way out of the hornets. He got pretty messed up and jumped in the water. Luckily he wasn't allergic so he survived.

Many believe the supernatural stir up mosquitoes and bees when humans overstep their boundary. Maybe it was just plain beginners luck... they didn't say it was always good! We had a great time and gained a little bit of tide on the Cobragator kraken and the sharks that killed all those escaped convicts! Be safe diving in the caves everyone, those are the true killers in that water.

CHAPTER 6
LAST ONES AT KOLOMOKI MOUNDS?

BLAKELY, GEORGIA

Kolomoki pyramid

America is home to many sacred prehistoric temples. Somehow these giant ancient structures were swept under the rug. I reign from

Ohio, land of 10,000 Mounds. I have always been interested in the mound builders, the sun worshippers. The Kolomoki Mounds in Georgia have been calling my name ever since I moved to the South and the hourglass was just about full. Sabrecat had a mountain of experiences and I was excited to join the ranks.

There are eight structures in the oldest and largest woodland site in the southeastern part of the country. There are burial, temple and ceremonial mounds. They align with the Summer Solstice and Winter Equinox. There is a museum built into one of the mounds. It provides an interesting look into the life of the mound builders. Sadly the museum was broken into and many of the artifacts were sold on the black market. A good portion were hunted down and returned but some are still in the wrong hands.

We pulled up to the front office and were ready to pay our admission when the lady told us the museum was closed. I was bummed we wouldn't be able to go inside the smaller temple mound but was excited to have the place to ourselves for the rest of the night. We pulled out of the HQ and stopped by the smaller mounds right down the road. I was impressed by the small ones, I was fumbling over myself to see the big one around the corner.

We pulled down the road and I saw the massive platform mound. The ancient vibrations were basically radiating off of the structure. We continued down the road and parked at the overnight camp house. We followed the path to the pyramid and I was in awe. I took a few pictures and tried to absorb as much of the energy in the air that I could.

We got to the staircase and made the steep climb. I latched onto the guard rail because I didn't want to fall and go stumbling down the unforgiving cement. That surely would have been painful. I'm sure I would have not been the first though. I followed the ninja as he took his time admiring the view. When I finally made it to the top, I felt like a king. I was on top of the world.

I explored the perimeter and took in the vibrations. The powerful frequencies created a barrier around this place. It was a perfect set up for defense and ceremony. The sun was going down while the moon was rising and we had a front row seat. We were magnets waiting to be matched with our opposite energy. I pulled out my EMF reader but it was acting up.

I made a video explaining some history of the place. I know that I probably only dipped my feet in the water. There is still an ocean of knowledge below my feet. Untapped frequencies and unanswered questions just waiting for the right alignment of energy and stars. Sabre found a path below and recommended that we go down and explore.

The sun was going down so I knew our time in the forest would be limited. We investigated some of the smaller mounds along the trail. There was a sign that showed some of the artifacts that were excavated from this area. There were small heads that reminded me of Mayan and Incan relics. The hairs on the back of my neck stuck up.

We followed the course and it became a dense woodland pretty quickly. There were tree bends and arches in every direction. I took a bunch of pictures and kept my eyes on a swivel. I was trying to tune into the language being spoken out here. Were they warnings or detailed messages about their family? I looked out for footprints but the foliage did a good job of masking the trace.

The cricket chorus was roaring so I still felt safe but I knew we were getting into uncharted territory. I didn't want to get too far off the main course because I knew we weren't alone out here. The mound was placed here for a reason. We need to tread lightly. We made it back out into the opening and noticed some cars acting suspicious by our truck.

We waited for them to pull off and then went to see if they stole anything out of the back. Saber was heated. He was not sure why they were messing with his car. Nothing was gone but what the heck were they doing. We checked under the hood and near his tires. We were on high alert cuz we knew the museum vandals could be lurking at any time. We weren't dealing with just normal lunatics, we were dealing with real life pirates.

After a while we decided to check out the last mound. We admired how they aligned with the summer solstice. We crossed the football field sized prairie and I fell into a trance. My legs kept moving forward but my mind was going back in time. I had visions of the people that built the mound. The children were running and playing. The women worked beside the tree line with baskets and cloth while the men hauled large rocks and logs. Some played ball games and others shot arrows. A tomahawk whistled past my head and I ducked down.

I heard the ninja laughing and I stepped out of the hallucination. We were approaching the round mound. The signs said to keep off and we followed the rules. We didn't want to fall into a subterranean chamber or pit to hell. We circled around the structure and soaked up the knowledge that it had on display. After a while of bliss, the ninja pointed back towards the temple mound and said he saw something moving on top of it.

I stared off into the distance and couldn't see much movement. I could sense that something was over there. The blanket of energy filled the prairie air quickly. I searched for shadow figures roaming above. I brought out my camera and started to zoom in. I made a video but couldn't spot anything. After a while of calm, we saw a bunch of deer run into the wood line. It wasn't them up there on the mound. What spooked them?

We marched back to the truck very quietly. We were being careful not to spook anything in the surrounding area. We were listening for a sign. The silence was deafening. I was ready to get back to the car and race to the state line. But when we made it back to the car, peace was flourishing. We ventured down to the creek and took a gander at the pond below. This place goes through phases and creates waves. I believe the structure has a strong connection to the moon. I will definitely be back.

CHAPTER 7
ALONE IN THE FLORIDA CAVERNS

MARIANNA, FL

Last one in the cave.

f I didn't work at the game store, I would definitely be a tour guide at the caverns. It's a spiritual feeling being underground and away from the static on the surface. The limestone and ancient fossils have their own vibrations. There are more than twenty-five cave systems in the park but the public only have access to one. I wonder what they are hiding. There have been many reports of hauntings and monstrous creatures lurking after dark so be careful on the only guided cavern tour in the Seminole state!

We pulled up to the state park and were happy to see the parking lot pretty empty. There was only one tour slot remaining for the evening and we were going to fill it up. We made it to the shop and bought the tickets. We had a half hour to explore the museum to get some background info.

We checked out the display cases of artifacts found in the park and the creatures we might encounter while underground.I told Sabre I did a tour at Squire Boone caverns back in the day. He was one of the only people that knew he was Daniel's brother. We watched a video in the theater and it timed up perfectly.

We walked down to the waiting area and our tour guide greeted us. He was a young Spanish guy that the park hired to do bilingual tours. We were the only two signed up for the excursion so we basically had the entire cavern to ourselves. That was both very cool but also pretty chilling. We could disappear down there or the lights could simply go out. Breathtaking...

The door was closed behind us and it was time to adventure. We brought up a story of a shadow figure captured on camera down here and our guide actually said that was on his tour. He told us a couple more stories that visitors have shared. Mostly orbs and blurs but strange sounds have come from some of the hidden tunnels. We had to keep a level head and watch our step but it may be our last!

The guide showed us the Wedding Cake in the Cathedral room. He pointed out a shark tooth and Sabrecat found a couple more. He showed us where snakes have climbed through and he pointed us to a sleeping bat. Some rocks were shaped as animals and others looked like faces. It felt like eyes were always watching us.

I asked him if he had seen the movies that were shot down here. He shook his head no but knew which ones I was talking about. I told him there had to be some roots in reality for the Cobragator and Sharkansas Women's Prison Massacre. These caves were home to some scary monsters in those movies and I feel it wasn't 100% fiction. He pointed us to the underground rivers and I could have sworn I saw some ripples!

We explored a spot called Frankenstein's Den. Killer vibes! He took us down the chamber of Short Man's revenge. I ducked down but the ninja banged his head pretty hard. I chuckled but knew it hurt. He stumbled but kept his cool. We kept moving forward until the room opened up with high ceilings. The gopher gang who dug this place out was highly impressive. I would have been claustrophobic! But no prey, no pay...

The guide asked if we wanted to experience total

darkness. Of course, we did. He turned the lights out for an extended amount of time and I slipped into the abyss. My mind went down the tunnels to the underworld. I bobbed and weaved between the pillars of Earth. I felt like I was Frodo in the Lord of the Rings. I could feel the Orcs working hard below, vibrating my feet. My eyes opened and it was still black.

I said alright... that's good and was met with silence. I reached for Sabre but felt nothing. I spun around and wanted to scream but couldn't. The air felt like it was sucked out of the room and I felt a pressure on my chest. I thought I was underwater and drowning. I opened my eyes again and the place was illuminated. The guys saw I was stunned and said the dark will play tricks on the mind. I could only shake my head up and down. I was trying to get back to normal breathing.

We took our time on the rest of the tour. It was a magical being in such a vast system. There was some space between each of us and no rush exploring. I'd make sure to take a glance down every nook and cranny. I was searching for those shadow creatures. I was looking for troglodytes or any sign from the other side. I know there are some hidden compartments that really open up down there. It might be an entrance to Agartha and this is one of the best chances we have to investigate it.

I was sad when we made it to the exit door. I wanted to run the tour back another time but the guide had already given us a good chunk of extra time. When we made it to the open air, the deep breaths were intoxicating. We scanned the area and remembered how it all looked before the storm. It is sad to see the destruction but I'm glad the caverns are back open again. I can't wait to explore the rest of the grounds and see what other secrets it holds! There are 27 other caves just in the state park, I have much more to explore!

We returned in the summer for the opening of the nature trail. The caves were incredible. They were a bit crowded but we still found our hidden Relief. Cam and Tristin led the way through the narrows and gallows as I peered around for the sabé and leprechaun people. We pointed out fossils and hidden faces in every room. Some truly reminded me of mud fossils. The vibes are truly special down there.

We turned onto the nature trail after the tour and our senses were tingling. After being underground for an hour, being exposed to the woods and sunlight was powerful. We could definitely see it being used in training and experiments. We heard strange noises but they were most likely deer and armadillos. The birds called out as we passed and we saw a black racer on the path. I can't wait to see what else is hiding at that park. The anomalies are attracted to the gopherwood tree planted in front!

CHAPTER 8
AFTER DARK AT THE LAKE JACKSON MOUNDS
LEON COUNTY, FLORIDA

The Major Mound

The prehistoric mounds in Tallahassee are something to behold. The ancient tribes picked the creekside haven for a reason and marked trees all around the mounds. There have been ghostly reports of Indian chants and growls from the swamp. The area is plagued with sinkholes so watch your step or it might be your last! We are trying to find the root of the Seminole! We are attempting to explain why these people abruptly abandoned this place!

Sabre scooped me and we stopped at the haunted Southern Express for a quick beverage and jerky stick. We passed Birchwood and I told him about the translucent creature that my friend Gilley witnessed. We stopped to visit the ghost town of Ocheesee and were back westbound. We crossed the Ochlockonee River and my goosebumps raised. I remembered the bigfoot beds being discovered farther down river. The water is a cryptid highway so I kept my eyes peered over the edge searching for a sign of anything!

We finally made it to the capital! We found the steep hill and knew we were close to the destination! We pulled up and within the first couple minutes at the park, we heard a chorus of loud cheers and cries. It sounded like a large group of girls were hosting a party over at the pavilion. I was wondering why they were there so late? When I stepped out of the bathroom, I asked Captain if he heard that too and he shook his head.

We crept forward and noticed a homeless man perched up on a blanket behind a bush near the creek. There was a book bag on the ground and his hands were full with clothes. It was highly suspicious. He locked his eyes on us as we walked past him toward the large mound. Whenever he had a clear path, he took off quickly out of the park. We had no clue if he was the source of those noises but it freaked me out a bit.

The sun was going down as we arrived at the mounds stairs. I took a couple steps and would pause to observe. I listened into the swamp and tried to spot any movement. We could feel a strange aura stemming from the dark. We knew something was over there. We explored in silence, waiting for a sign.

After a while, we climbed down and wanted to investigate the creek. We followed a path and came upon some barn ruins. It seemed like it was someone's property. We crept around and heard a loud noise in the forest. As we looked up, we jumped two huge deer that took off in an instant. We made it back to the park and the sunlight was beginning to dim.

We maneuvered around the giant muddy puddles but our shoes still got dirty. We made it over to the smaller mound and walked up the backside of it. I took some pictures before it got too dark. I sat on the steps and absorbed the ancient vibrations. I tried to join in on their smiles and cries. I imagined all the different uses of the area. I attempted to place my mind in the chief's mental state. I wanted to see what our home used to be.

We hiked the perimeter, searching for tracks or anything out of place. The sky was dark and the vibe was getting creepy. We heard more rustling in the forest but it could have been anything. We stopped and froze a handful of times but we didn't feel threatened at all. We felt a car coming down the hill and sure enough it was a security guard. We backed into the shadows and made our way to the truck. The staff went straight to the bathrooms and were not worried about us.

Water trees.

Our duo headed out and had our heart beating for a second. I had to go to the restroom and didn't get a chance to go coz of the rush. We made it out of busy Tallahassee and stopped at Gretna for some relief, snacks and beer. This gas station is a known hot spot for danger. I heard a story that a hooker entered a man's car while he was inside paying. Other stories of people being robbed in the back of the restrooms. I had to go so bad that I didn't care and Ninja had my back.

We cruised out and crossed the timeline above the

swamp. We pulled off the highway and stopped at Ocheesee Landing. This spot was supposed to be the Florida capital and now it is a ghost town! I showed him where my mom and I found bigfoot tracks and even pointed out the secret geocache hidden at the base of the famous oak tree. Shiver me timbers!

I told him about the recent encounter that a man had while fishing at the landing. He heard a sasquatch scream from across the river. Then it emerged from the forest and continued to intimidate the fisherman. He quickly left and is pretty shaken up by it. He wouldn't even directly talk to me. I heard the story from a couple that is best friends with him. They grew up over there and know the wildman lurks!

We looked for one more roadside geocache but had no luck. Either it was moved by the storm or stolen by crooks! Might be the faeries, might be the Jerry's. We pulled onto my street and crept slowly past the abandoned haunted trailer behind my spot. I always look in the windows and try to find clues to the other side.

We enjoyed the rest of the night with conspiracy convoys and fishing videos. He showed me different techniques on hitting my punching bag and I showed him how much some of my Pokémon cards were worth. I really need to bust out my N64 soon and we can seek enlightenment through Dark Rift and Turok. We are real life dinosaur hunters!

CHAPTER 9
CHATTAHOOCHEE LANDING MOUNDS
GADSDEN COUNTY, FL

Hurricane torn boardwalk.

F or some odd reason, when you search for prehistoric Panhandle structures, this gem is hard to find. Luckily if you follow the sacred river, you run right into these ancient mounds. Not far from the colossal gators in Lake Seminole, there is one giant temple mound and six smaller structures in a semi circle around it. They align with the Summer solstice and Winter equinox. The energy there lives forever. Energy is never created nor destroyed. There are many other cool points in the park and region that are worth checking out.

Before we crossed the river, the ninja pulled off on a dirt road to show me an uncharted spot. He said this place was known as dead man's valley and this is where people used to dump bodies back in the day. He said there was a good chance there are some undiscovered John Doe's in this swamp. I made a video and we navigated the muddy roads. We pulled under the original Victory Bridge and kept an eye out for hobos and cool graffiti. Magical spot.

We hopped back in the truck and made it to the landing. I admired the smaller mounds as we pulled in. We also passed an oven that the British troops dug out in the landscape. We parked the car and began to explore the riverbank. We were looking for dead fish, animal tracks and cool fossils. We saw some crayfish and some bass jumping in the distance. This bank was famous for fallen ships. We found some cool wreckage!

We cut up towards the forest and noticed a path that led to a walkway. The boardwalk was badly damaged. There were trees fallen and the bottom was beginning to rot out. It was a perfect place to risk it for the biscuit. The foot traffic in the past few months had to be very low so we might surprise something back there. There was a strong magnetism coming from the bush, basically whispering our name.

Shinobi said the path was quite magical in its prime. We pushed forward and climbed over every obstacle in our way. The boards cracked on a couple different occasions and I had to step quickly and lightly at the same time. It would have been about a ten foot fall into the murky water full of jagged wood. I rather not be snake bait.

I took a handful of photos and videos back there. I was sure we had some eyes on us. We were making quite a bit of noise because the path was completely covered in leaves. Sabre held his hand up ahead and I stayed back where I was about forty feet behind him. He had his head on a swivel and signaled to move forward. He later told me that he heard something whizz past our head. Was it a large bug or was something thrown at us? Or maybe shot?

We continued until the path totally collapsed. We climbed down and jumped to land. We followed the animal tracks in the mud. After a while we noticed a dirt maintenance road up ahead. We hiked that until we noticed a deer blind up ahead. We did not want to spook any hunters or get caught on trail cam so we fell back.

We got back on the walkway and started back toward the park. We heard some splashing in the water behind some trees but never got a visual on the target. It could have been a large turtle or maybe just a big fish. Even

Edward Bloom would be a little bit alarmed and he's friends with a giant! We made it back to land and were pulled to the mound like a magnet.

The Mound

We circled around the circle soaking in the energy. I snapped a few photos using my old friend Wolf's trick. The key to catching orbs is to look away from the camera screen when taking the picture. I don't think there were too many camera anomalies this time but the vibes were definitely there. We marched through the field to the oven and I was just amazed.

We trekked up the primary temple mound. We sat on top and watched the river. I imagined the Scott Massacre but understood both sides to the story. More than thirty people lost their lives. This place will always have tremors. I went further back and soaked in the solstice rituals the ancient people would practice. The moon was beaming and I knew that meteor showers and eclipses would bring this place to life.

I'm sure the raven mockers could see us clearly and well from across the river. The water is sacred. Littered with dead bodies, ancient fossils and brackish fish. Sea serpents and cave eels are the rare killers. The common crook is the monster gators that patrol the deep waters along the dam. They say there are man sized catfish down there too. Reminds me of the Ohio River! I'm sure they have the Mantis Man too!

We made our way down the pyramid and ran over to the Victory Bridge. This was once part of the intercoastal highway that went from St. Augustine all the way to San Diego! They tore down the original bridge and built a new one. The remnants of the original still stand and are blocked off by barbed wire fences. We climbed up to the fence and took some pictures. Too many freaking cars to hop the spikes that night…

We took our time back to the car. We admired the oven and the mounds. I tried to sink back into ancient frequencies before we left. The forest and the river spoke to me. So many people have traversed this jungle on a quest for more. If they were aiming for the Gulf, they would be there in no time. It wouldn't be long til thar she blows! Landlubbers marooned!

Just watch out for the banks, there's some haunted forts and steep bluffs with eyes on you. The murky waters hold known reptiles and serpents but the cracks are home to something much more sinister. Brackish water attracts the baddest monsters. The fossils of saber tooth tigers and rhinoceros attract rare vibrations. Sync in or get sunk.

CHAPTER 10
HOODED SASQUATCH OF FALLING WATERS
CHIPLEY, FLORIDA

Michael Myers mural. Jackson County, Florida.

alling Waters is definitely something to see but the feeling it provided might remain stained forever. The hundred foot waterfall plunges deep into a sinkhole and the vibrations it gives off are intoxicating. There is a lake and a trail that weaves through steep terrain and more sinkholes! A caped cryptid was spotted recently so keep your head on a swivel or it might be the last time you visit a state park!

Many years ago, they were searching for black gold in this region. The seekers had to watch over their shoulder for mountain lions, bears, and angry boar but the poisonous snakes and monsters in the caves were the primary predators. The abundance of resources and intersection of ley lines attracts all forms of life. Life thrives below the surface, throughout the campground, and the skies above! You can just feel the history oozing out of the region...

It had been raining all week, so I figured there wouldn't be a better time to visit the most famous water-fall in Florida. I was lucky enough to visit the park with my neighbors the year before. I was enthralled by all the natural beauty and really wanted to return for a picnic one day. Well, no blanket and basket today, but it was time to do a deep dive in the sinkhole capital of the sunshine state!

I parked my car at the shop and waited for Captain to slide through. On the way toward Chipley, I asked if we could check out the abandoned nuke silos in town. I recently saw drone footage and noticed some wild horror themed paintings. I needed to see Michael Myers first hand. And to my surprise, when we pulled up, Freddy and Jason were waiting for us too. Snoopy and some bird thangs too!

I made a video narrating my excitement and exploring the insides. The ground was covered in feces and you could hear the birds and bats squeaking above. There was tons of other cool graffiti and sadly garbage everywhere. I even saw some used needles. I wiped off my shoes and shook my head. What a magical place, people just need to show some respect. My video got more than a thousand likes on Tiktok and nearly 7k views. Definitely something to see.

We hopped back on the road and passed the haunted mansions of Marianna. I stared into the windows as we drove by. I always keep my eyes peeled for movement or light beams. We followed 90 all the way until Chipley. We kept an eye out for deer crossing the road out of this dense forest. I pointed out the disc golf course on our right. I'd pay good money to see the ninja line up with his putter.

As we got closer, I told ninja about the sasquatch encounter that was reported here. I told him that a woman spotted a dark figure hiding behind a tree. The creature was stalking her and her dog while she was hiking the trail. The beast seemed to be wearing a hooded cape. It truly reminded me of the Flatwoods Monster. There are

We pulled up to the park and my eyes were wide. There were two giant school busses in the parking lot.

They were tagged @ourvanlife and That Miller Life. I grabbed one of my books and ran over to them. I wanted to introduce myself to some fellow travelers.

I knocked on the door and two nice women opened up. They were a little surprised but once I got my introduction out of the way, they were very welcoming. I told the madames that I was a cryptid researcher and I was investigating the recent sasquatch sighting. I gave them a copy of Erie Swamps. They were friendly corsairs.

Jake rolled up on a scooter wondering if I was a scourge. I was not trying to pillage and he sensed that, then dapped me up. We shared each other's stories and really bonded. I wish I would have invited him along but the rain was picking up and the mission was covert. I wish I at least got a picture with them and the bus. I took off down the trail with my senses heightened.

We stopped by the butterfly garden and took a look at the map. After we scanned the area, we hopped on the boardwalk toward the waterfall. We ran into Abe and said what's up to him and his son. We told him to keep his eyes peeled for the skunk ape and he said he was. He did some sick drone work down into the sinkhole that I saw later. It was rad.

We climbed down the stairs and the sound of the falling water was serene. We absorbed the mist and stared down into the sinkhole. I imagined what it would be like to fall down there. Then I visualized the group effort it would take to pull someone out from the deep hole. I became the water in my mind and flowed into the aquifer. I enjoyed the underground ocean until I snapped back to reality.

We enjoyed the cascade for a bit and then decided to hit the trail. The forest was blanketed in mist. It was a perfect setting for a predator to lurk in the shadows. We tried to pay attention to the birds and squirrels for tips. The rain masked most of the light sounds but we could still hear some rustling in the distance. We spotted a couple deer and even saw some coyote tracks.

We made it to the pond and circled the perimeter, looking for some alligators. We saw a bunch of cool tracks on the beach but no slide marks. We kept an eye out for snakes and log turtles. I sparked a gross roach blunt and knew the strong smell would attract some curiosity. My dirty buzz paid off as I was able to slip into a stupor. I was able to read between the lines of the area. I felt like a bat using echolocation.

I mapped the sinkholes in my mind and the pillars of Earth came to life. The prowlers from the movie The Descent were surely under our feet. I imagine they are very sensitive towards vibrations and frequencies. They would know when intruders get close to their entrances. I wondered if the nearby Rock Preserve and possible volcano were linked to what was happening over here.

The rain was coming down hard now and we still had more to explore. We followed the trail to the popular sinkhole and climbed down for a closer look. We had to cross a small natural bridge and watch our step on both sides. The water was rushing below our feet and just one misstep could be fatal. We yelled down into the holes, hoping for a response. As we turned back, a strange feeling leaked from below. It wasn't a growl but it surely was a presence.

State park

We hustled back to the car and shook off our goose-bumps. We wondered if it were a sasquatch below our feet or something much larger. I visualized cthulhu, Godzilla or the kaiju from Pacific Rim rumbling below. The sinkholes may even be entrances to Middle Earth or portals to forbidden continents. We debated theories on our way through town.

I made a video outside of Washington County News and told the story of the original owner that still shows up everyday to work...in ghost form! I pointed out the haunted tower of the library and stopped at a pawn shop. We were still soaking wet. We made one last stop at the Green Oaks mansion in Greenwood to snap some pictures. I wanted to see if I could capture any orbs or strange faces...

CHAPTER 11
LOT GOING ON AT TORREYA STATE PARK
LIBERTY COUNTY, FLORIDA

Campsite 4, hot spot.

Torreya State Park has it all! Breathtaking views, bigfoot legends, Civil War forts and even a haunted mansion! The hurricane tore the grounds apart but the park's perseverance shines strong.

Make sure you are out before sundown, the gate closes automatically! Enjoy the pristine lands and peaks, there's no other place anything like it in the Sunshine State!

Large footprint

Our original plan was to explore the Big Bend Jai Alai arena but sadly things changed. When we arrived in Chattahoochee, work crews were still active on the grounds and trespassing signs were posted in all directions. We made a short video before we drove off.

Sabercat was really paranoid that the cops would be called. I wanted to at least ask if we could take some pictures up close. Guess I'd have to wait for another day.

We chose to hit up Torreya instead. I was very excited coz I had been up and down the river but hadn't visited the park yet. I knew all about the famous Gregory House that used to sit at Ocheesee Landing. I have visited the old grounds countless times but it was time for me to climb the hill.

We pulled into the park and went straight to the river. Sabre noticed the automatic gate and sign that read that it closes at sundown. It was getting late but the sun was still up for now. We had a lot to explore with not much time. But honestly I didn't believe the gates would automatically close so I wasn't stressing it one bit.

The haunted Gregory House.

We pulled up to the Gregory house and admired its beauty. The clay brick walkway leading up to the mansion was breathtaking. We recorded a short video about the history of the place and began exploring. The house was closed but we still peaked in the windows and absorbed the vibes. On TikTok, a viewer noticed the curtains moving while I was talking in the video. There was definitely nobody in the house so it must have been a ghost!

We made it to the back of the house and were intoxicated by the setting. The tree tops and Apalachicola River were a sight to see. I imagined all the creatures crawling below. So much history, so little coverage. This region was blanketed with anomalies and most never see the light of day.

We followed a trail into the woods and explored the Civil War locations that were marked along the trail. I closed my eyes and envisioned the olden days. Hiding out in forts, aiming at the river. Swatting at mosquitoes and dodging venomous snakes. The alligator and bore were at least big enough that you'd hear them coming. The size and speed of a clipper though...

We made another short video discussing the bigfoot sightings in the area. I talked about how Stacy Brown and his father captured the best civilian thermal footage of a sasquatch and that the Ocheesee Pond Wildman's ancestors still roam these lands. I also mentioned the Garden of Eden trail and how it may be a sacred soul.

Twenty-seven of the twenty-eight trees mentioned in the Bible are in the region. Noah used gopherwood to build the ark and it's also known as toreya. The only place it grows is this state park! You can be the judge!

We found a giant footprint that may have belonged to a bigfoot. We took pictures and kept our eyes peeled. A silence swept the forest and we took that as our cue to leave. The sun was going down and we did not want to get stuck here. We heard a car making the rounds and figured the park was closing. We made it out of the canopy and began jogging to our car. We were pedaling to the metal when we noticed the gate was closing.

Sabre floored it and the future envisioned right before my eyes. I could see the gate closing in on us and flipping our car. Then we would have been arrested for the property damage. Luckily I screamed to stop and Ron slammed on his breaks. We came to a screeching halt just inches from the metal. We definitely wouldn't have made it. Luckily the ranger watched it all unfold and opened the gate for us.

We went to Ruby Tuesday's for dinner and washed down our fear with beer. The employees asked us what our adventure was this time and we told them. One man came to the bar and acted like he knew it all. He was judging us because the waitresses were more interested in our stories than his compliments. When I went to the bathroom, I guess he was staring at Captain. We left shortly after. He wasn't worth the trouble. We can take on goblins, demons, and monsters but I got no energy for a non believer.

We returned to the park on April 14, and had a bone chilling experience. We passed the timeline and were suddenly an hour closer to the park closing. It was sprinkling and the skies were a strange gray. We looked for some gems and then pulled into the ranger station. We asked about primitive camping and what time the gates would close.

Our conversations led to bigfoot encounters around the park. He told us that Camp 4 at Rock Creek primitive camp was a popular spot for anomalies. Sabre knew the direction so we were off. We told the guy we would be back in May for the anniversary of the Brown footage. Rest in Peace Mr. Brown.

We pulled around the corner and we checked the truck bed for the turtle that Captain saved earlier. We walked past the playground. We took off down the trail and I set up my go pro headset. I sparked an L and we were jet set radio. We discussed the local stories and looked for tracks as we drove deeper into the forest. I kept an ear out for anything that rang a certain vibration. I was really feeling out of the woods because I knew its history.

We heard some owl hoots from a distance. A hoot from a sasquatch just sounds different. The path was serene. We kept our eyes forward, alert for snakes or more importantly ground glyphs. Sometimes the forest people will leave clues or signs on the path that could play as a warning or communication with other tribes. There is a realm of existence well beyond everyday human understanding.

We made it to the campgrounds and were sitting on one of the small benches around the unlit fire pit. We mistook it for number four but it didn't matter because within the first couple minutes we were climbing below us. It was trampling in the creek just past a huge patch of brush. I was frozen because I had a good feeling of what it was.

I just wanted to sit still and put my ear toward the presence. We were in a vulnerable spot, a good hike back to safety and the rain was picking up. I was not prepared to sprint back through the valley of death. We attempted a couple openings but they were roads blocked by deadfall. At that point the creature would have been gone or waiting with a trap to see if we were dumb enough to put ourselves in such a vulnerable position.

May 12, we returned for another hike. We crossed a broken bridge and were in the deep thicket. We had a large boulder thrown near the trail about twenty yards behind us. We remained calm but needed to get out of there. We were delirious from the heat and running low on fluids. We ended up meeting with Tristin from Hidden Relief. We took some pictures and checked out Campsite 4. Lot different vibe than last time near the creek.

Of course when reviewing the footage at half speed, we found strange figures following us in the woods. One resembled a symbiote like Venom and Carnage in the tree. Another looked just like a wolf, a very tall one and the other looked just like Patty from the Bluff Creek footage. Donnie had a face to face encounter days later on the challenge bridge.

It's amazing how low key they remain in their realm, they are truly incognito. We have all encountered cryptids. They got us ready with the Easter Bunny and Santa so we would be ready for bigfoot and mothman. The caveman is always plotting but so do the pirates!

CHAPTER 12
GOATMAN OF COHEELEE CREEK
BLAKELY, GEORGIA

Under the bridge

T he Coheelee Creek Covered Bridge is one of the most historic places in Southern Georgia. The 1800s wooden structure stretches over the raging creek and waterfall below. The soil is soaked with history and the beams still hold strong. There is a dark past of crime in the area and a mysterious beast seeks retribution for the unjust past. Beware of the Goatman while visiting Blakely, or you're gonna be bucked.

There are many Goatman legends across the planet. My mind goes directly to centaurs and the legend of Lake Worth. I know Kentucky and Maryland had famous stories too. The creatures were known as faun in ancient times. They appeared in Spyro, Pan's Labyrinth, and Chronicles of Narnia. But of course Baphomet is the most famous goatman. Well, him and Black Phillip. I also interviewed a policeman who witnessed a goatman on Halloween morning in Bainbridge. That is just a hoof and a horn's toss away!

I was fresh off an all nighter with Lucy and a podcast with Gypsy Road when Captain hit me up to adventure. The moon was bright and the vibes were calling to us. If October was the eighth month like it's supposed to be, then tonight would have been Christmas Eve. It was the perfect night to call Krampus, we were heading to Georgia to see the Goatman!

I left my car at Ruby Tuesday's and hopped in the monster truck. We headed north and kept our eyes out for deer. We made it to Greenwood and admired the historic mansions. I quickly looked for ghost stories but sadly couldn't find any. Bigcat fixed his mirror and noticed someone was tailing us. We took a few weird turns and they were still on us. What the heck did they want?

We pulled into a church and they luckily kept cruising. I felt like I was in the opening scene of Jeepers Creepers. As darkness fell, we crept towards the closed park. My mind was racing and I had chills thinking of the beast. I felt like I had been here before, somewhere deep in my nightmares. Each breath felt more and more familiar. Like deja vu…

We pulled up to the backside of the bridge and my heart was pounding out of my chest. We opened up our doors and could hear the water rushing below. Sabrecat rushed out while I was fumbling through my bag. I heard a strange sound over my shoulder and in the woods. I knew this place was special when the goosebumps hit my ankles. Finally found my lighter and spliff, then caught up at the river.

The water was raging below and you could feel a strange energy surrounding us in the forest. We admired and tried to decipher the graffiti. I lit my blunt below the bridge in a nice secluded area. I knew the smell would attract anything in the area. Soon we felt curious eyes glued to our movement. We were not alone out there. We noticed the light was flickering across the bridge. We were surrounded by all realms of existence.

We adventured along the creek and decided to check out the park on the other side. We stopped to investigate the landing on the river before we made the trek to the other side. I reminded the ninja of all the bodies found in the same river after the Atlanta murders. We had a moment of silence and appreciation before we circled back to the covered bridge park.

Blocked off access

We pulled up and the light began to flicker immediately. Then we heard a yell from towards the river. Two cries to be exact. I wanted to record a short video discussing the history of the place but we were having trouble with the lighting. We tried to pull his truck up with the bright lights but nothing was working. We gave up on the video and explored the grounds. As we walked, something paced us from beyond the shadows. Stu said he saw some eyes in the woods.

We climbed under the bridge and looked for animal tracks. We spotted more graffiti and some had strange symbology. If we slipped in the water, there would be a good chance we would not survive. Every step was very careful. We could barely see and the mist was multiplying by the minute. I figured we had one more shot at the video so we went back to the other side and shined our bright lights. Luckily we captured some quality footage and highlighted the history.

We headed out of there shortly after. The layer of unknown still lingered on our clothing. Stu's truck was sputtering and we needed gas. We finally found a station and were met with mean mugs from the locals. We escaped unharmed and were back on the road. Ron dropped me off at my car and then we stopped at the gas station to grab some brews. He followed me home and on the last turn, the watchers struck.

As I pulled into my yard and shut off my car, sirens surrounded me. Four sheriff SUV's poured into my grass and barricaded me in. I opened up my car door and they screamed at me not to leave the vehicle. I put my hands up and was ready to cooperate. I was not sure what I did wrong. I was not sure if someone called the cops on me or if I was being arrested for trespassing in my previous videos.

H for Hell?

They took my ID and told me that I took the left hand turn too fast. They questioned me if I had been drinking and I told them I was exploring in Georgia. They asked me why my friend in the white truck drove away. I told them that he didn't like confrontations and bright lights bothered him. They searched my name and let me be.

They told me that I had a light out above my license plate but they were definitely fishing. But luckily I had nothing to hide.

I scurried inside and let my cats know that I was alright. They were alarmed by all the commotion outside. This was the second time I have been pulled over for a sub par reason on my street. I am beginning to believe that it has more to do with the places I'm investigating than my driving. I called Sabrecat and told him the coast was clear.

He rolled over a couple minutes later and we discussed our night. I was still shaking from my backyard encounter. We drank a couple beers and watched some outdoor adventure videos. We drew connections between the night and our first adventure at Bellamy Bridge. The correlations were uncanny. There was a strange energy that definitely latched itself onto the visitors. The coffer keeper was definitely protecting something important.

Captain was nervous that the house was still under surveillance when he left. He went the back way and luckily made it home safely. He did say he saw a lot of deer out that night. Hours later, I finally passed out and was back at the creek. This time the barriers didn't exist and I was able to walk across the bridge. As I walked slowly, I felt a warm presence guiding me along. The Goatman was near!

CHAPTER 13
CRYSTAL FROG CAVERN
CAVEMAN
JACKSON COUNTY, FLORIDA

First time in the cave.

My legs are still sore and my good pair of shoes are covered in mud but we had one hell of a night. Sabre told me a couple months ago about a cave that multiple people have tragically drowned in. Last time he visited, he heard children's voices, laughing and playing. I knew I had to investigate it and finally the time had come.

We parked at a safe location and walked along the highway for a while. We dipped down the side and under a bridge. We made it to the railroad. Our target was more than three miles eastward and we had to make sure we stayed out of sight because they took walking the tracks pretty seriously around town. We were dressed in dark clothes and saved the flashlight for when we were underground or truly in the middle of nowhere. Sadly I wore my Nike skate shoes. I couldn't find my all terrain New Balance. Every step was met with resistance on that path. Three felt like thirteen.

We came across a bunch of dead turtles. They climb over part of the railroad and then just follow one direction until they either get run over or die from dehydration. The metal gets really hot during the day. Luckily for us, the night started cool and calm but I can definitely understand how the turtle can get locked inside the tunnel of trance. I was nervous I wouldn't hear a train approaching. Unexplainable things happen everyday.

We jumped a couple of animals. Some sounded like coyotes and deer but one was much slower moving. It smelled like thick pine. Like a cow or horse. Big and strong. Not a bad stink but powerful to alert your nose.

We never felt threatened but my sixth sense told me that something big was nearby. Maybe it was a gator, maybe it was the Creature from Black Lagoon.

We had to duck down and the army crawled on the tracks at one point. Headlights shined on us for a couple of seconds and then turned when we kept walking. Sabre said it was most likely a hunter checking on his property. We kept a good pace and after a while it was a distant memory. We crossed a couple high bridges and it was peaceful looking over the swamp. I knew there were many eyes on us.

We heard some strange noises while walking and had to stop a couple of times. I'm sure the nearby forest was used by visitors. Maybe some homeless traveling the tracks and dangerous poachers. They were probably confused about our energy and just curious about what we were up to. I thought I heard a cough just off the ridge. After that I picked up a railroad spike for protection. I knew we were being followed.

Finally Captain said we were there. I hopped off the railroad and followed him into the woods. Sadly everything looked the same and we were having major trouble finding the spot. He pushed through the briar and stomped over branches. I had my head on a swivel. I was not trying to be blindsided and whisked away into one of these deep caverns. Not today's Beetlejuice. I asked for help from t

We circled back a couple times and finally located the treasure. He flashed the light on a fence that had been pushed over. He said that bears had come and knocked it down while burrowing in the caves. We climbed through the gap and down the steep dirt hill into the mouth of the cave. He was hesitant and told me to be ready for a creature down below. I had my knife ready for a panther or bear but if it was a hobbit or gremlin, I might surrender.

Spooky grafitti

We crawled in and heard a couple things jump into the water. The place was filled with bats, frogs, and of course snakes but I felt right at home. I perched up on a rock after falling twice but I was good. My ankle hurt but in the moment, I was surrounded by ancient vibes and crystal water. I peaked down and envisioned all the places the cracks lead to.

Visions of Godzilla and cobragators flooded my cranium. This hole in the rock was a heavenly stadium. The visitors of this sacred spot were in a special club and I was so honored to join. The vibes blanketed our bodies and my glasses were fogging up. I sparked a blunt and shared my smoke with anybody still down there. A fog was created and it surely looked magical above the water. The reflection was so clear that you couldn't tell where the water began. It was trippy.

I snapped out of trance when I heard a loud train horn. I swear it shook the rocks below or just the inside of my chest. I looked over to ninja and he had heard it too. We waited patiently for a train to pass but it never came. That was weird. He said that was the ghost train. We have heard it a couple times around town now. It reminded me of back home at River Styx and Cry Baby Bridge.

I was covered in mud but my soul was cleansed. It felt good to share that time underground with the bats and water. I tried to remember the ones who passed away there. Hopefully one day I will be scuba trained and can dive down to see what they were looking for. If I ever return during the day, I'm going to bring my snorkel gear to see what else is down there. Many secrets of the past are just a couple feet below us everyday. It's truly fascinating. We named the cave Crystal Frog Cavern.

Skunk Ape track found during the Void Cat

We crawled out of the oasis and it felt like the temperature dropped fifteen degrees. We adventured under the tracks for a bit and found some cool graffiti of a ghost. We shined the light in the overflow and found a bunch of crayfish! There were some minnows and we saw one exotic looking fish. We weren't able to ID it but it felt like we were meant to see it. Truly magical.

We climbed back up onto the tracks and the wind was blowing hard. This was going to be a long trek back.

Luckily we joked about movies and urban legends, making time pass by. We used to light up on the way back and found a couple cool gems. Sabre of course found some gold and a cool skeleton of a serpent. That strange smell was gone when we returned. It definitely wasn't the trees.

We could finally see the bridge ahead and cars passing by. We stayed down and climbed up the steep drop-off. We made it to the road and now we were clear and cool. If anybody asks, we were at the gas station playing the lottery. Haha!

Sabre picked up some food while I grabbed the beers. I was nervous on the way home because my tag light was still out and now I feel like the dang sheriffs are watching me every time I turn into town. A white SUV followed me until the last turn but luckily I made it to my yard without the blue and red sirens.

I ran inside and was happy to see Kodak and Cudi. I turned on Survivorman Bigfoot and started to roll up. Couple minutes later, the ninja pulled up and we reminisced about the night. We were both dead tired and delirious from the day but still drowning in laughter. We turned on a ghost box and got some interesting responses. The audible words were knife, niece, boat, trapped, bloody and what. Pretty spooky stuff. He left at three am and the rest is history. My back still burns.

I returned back to the cave in the daytime months

later. We had to show Tristin the magical spot... While resting after the strenuous journey, I was digging in the dirt and found a meteorite. It was just days after my friend discovered one and I manifested it in my mind. Thoughts become reality when we push the distractions aside. We were greeted by our amphibian friend and everything seemed right in the world. Well at least in the dark cave...

———

Weeks later.. I've been hiking, meditating, and sleeping with this magnetic rock. It has been enhancing my energy and making my dreams go crazy. The world's static seems to dissipate when I can really channel the gem's vibration. I am not the first person to find this stone and I will not be the last. I will be leaving it on an upcoming expedition. We will see where it ends up...

Returned again with Jack to work on our short film. We are entered into a Halloween film festival in Tallahassee! I can't wait to see it on the big screen but something happened underground! We found a footprint with five clear toes! We took pictures and video of it and I'm going to try to get back to plaster cast it! Something was down there with us. I had a strange feeling and announced ourselves before we went fully down. I think that may have saved us.

Casted the print the next day with the walking

legend. The final product came out perfect and now I'm addicted to the plaster! So excited to find more tracks and evidence! Swamp thing or feral railroad people. Either way it was pretty cool...and scary! Beware of the caveman!

CHAPTER 14
HUNTING THE PENSACOLA SERPENT IN PANAMA
BAY COUNTY, FL

Hathaway Bridge, Bay County, Florida.

T he Gulf of Mexico is home to many secrets and sunken treasures. Buccaneers, explorers, and refuges have all flocked to the large pond. There have been stories of giant sea creatures, UFO bases, and crashed planes through the region. Earthquakes and severe pollution have also stirred the pot of possibilities in America's bath. I have been visiting the mysterious source of water since I was a child, something is always pulling me back. Maybe one of these days, I'll figure it out, but until then, I'll just keep treading.

I had a day off and the ninja had the fishing itch. I was dying to smell the salt water and my soul was yearning to enter the abyss again. He recommended setting up under the Hathaway Bridge and I was down. It just so happened to be the week of the fifty-ninth anniversary of the Pensacola Serpent incident. The stars had aligned and it was time to investigate the gulf waters. Some people have never seen the saltwater, take a look through my eyes....

It was time for the pirates to take on the kraken. On Wednesday night, we did some local exploring. We adventured along the Chipola, checking out Look and Tremble rapids. I told the ninja about the religious snake handlers that used to dwell in these woods. They tested their holiness with venomous serpents and some were not as pure as they believed. There was also an incident amongst a group of robbers that turned on each other and killed one another back here too. He told me about the gators and cottonmouths he had encountered while kayaking the rapids. We had a blast looking for fossils and gold. We even saw a grey fox!

We stopped at Johnny Boy landing and had a

moment of silence at the grave. We shine our lights across the water and down the flooded creek. We crept through a path into the woods until it came to an abrupt stop. Our buddy Dylan's family witnessed a black panther drinking from the river down here. We were ready for anything. We went back to my house and watched some Miller Wilson fishing videos. We decided we would hit the gulf the next afternoon.

I just started a movie and was halfway through a roach blunt when my phone rang. He asked if I was still down to fish and I told him of course. I ran over to my mom's house and grabbed some equipment. She gave me two rods, a net and her tackle box. She's always prepared. Sometimes I take that for granted. I thanked her and hurried back to my trailer because the white truck was waiting.

I took a dab, grabbed some gummies and we were off to the Emerald Coast, to the most beautiful beaches on the face of known Earth. We stopped by the haunted funeral home on Sherry Street and got a bit turned around. We got back on track and onto 231. We crossed Bear Creek and I told Sabre about the 1972 bigfoot sighting. Four boys were camping a half mile from the road and two of them saw a giant grey figure right after making a boogeyman joke. I always keep my eyes peeled.

As we got into town, we could tell it was spring break from all the chaos. Golf carts were everywhere and tourists flooded the sidewalks. I love to see happy faces and bright lights. The upside down Wonderworks building, Ripley's, and all the wild golf courses. I imagined the dinosaurs and giant creatures coming to life and chasing the muggles.

We adventured into Walmart to get the ninja his license and some bait. They didn't have squid but they had boneless wings. We drove around town and stopped at three gas stations and convenience marts but they didn't have jack squat. We found a half hitch and got some perfect stinky bait. We threw some ice in the cooler and parked beside the bridge.

We carried our equipment down some steep rocks and set up between the overpasses. We made a couple trips and said what's up to the guy throwing the cast net. I was excited to get some bait on my hooks and into the water. But sadly it didn't take long for me to figure out the conditions were rough. It was windy as heck and the waves were running.

I set up my two rods in my chair and went out on an adventure.

Under the overpass, was a bunch of sharp rocks that boarded the water. There was cool graffiti and more importantly, a perfect place to blaze. I sat beside the salt water and puffed away on my delta 8 and mids mixture. I ate my handful of gummies and was enjoying myself for quite a while. I remembered the Pensacola incident. I envisioned the serpent climbing out like in the movie The Host.

Fifty-nine years ago, five guys were diving on the USS Massachusetts. They encountered horrible weather and ended up holding onto a buoy for dear life. After dreadful days, the boys were hunted by a giant creature. One by one, the boys were swallowed up. Only one survived to tell the story. The news covered it up but there are still many tales throughout the Gulf. Many sunken ships and reports of UFOs and UAPs entering and emerging from the water.

On my way back from my new spot, I overexerted myself and a headache kicked my butt. I was feeling dizzy and worn out, while dodging snakes. It didn't make sense. I had food in my belly and drank some Powerade. I've learned my lesson too many times against dehydration. This was different. I figured it was a low quality mixture of herbs. Bummer.

I sat down in the chair and tried to breathe it out. I threw some more casts and was pushing through the pain. Ninja grabbed a net and used some of his ninjutsu skills to use it. He used the light from the road above and snagged some blinded fish. He caught about six and we let them go. They might have been good for bait but it was cool to just see them on the net.

We stayed for another hour with not much luck on the rod and reel. We decided to check out the pier. I was hesitant because my head was pounding but it was one of my favorite spots and I was optimistic about it healing me. I should have stopped for some medicine but figured my Powerade would help do the trick. I was wrong.

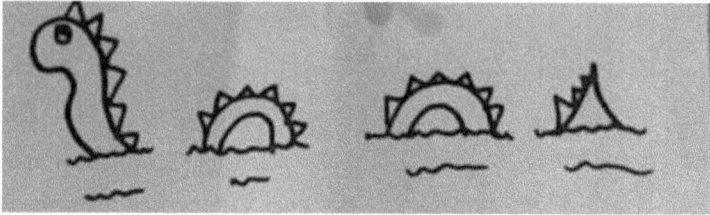

The monster we're hunting

We carried our equipment down the long pier. The stars were out and the night was perfect. I was mad at myself that I was feeling so poorly. I have to break free from this gulf slump that I have been in. Last deep sea trip I went on, I was puking my stomach bile. I shouldn't have eaten the oysters the night before but the waves were choppy. Half the boat was in the infirmary.

I pushed through the pain and set up on the end of the pier. We saw some people catching nice sized sailcats so I was confident about our chances. I tossed my bait in the water and curled up on the bench. I was sweating but I was cold. The wind was blowing in my face and up my pant leg. I was trying to soak up the moon light and wished upon a star for healing.

Ninja had some eighties music playing and I started to feel a bit better. I had a good laugh when I noticed a green laser beaming down from one of the hotels. I shined my light and tried to do my own Connor's code language. I tried my best to tough it out but the wind was brutal. I think I was able to fall asleep for a little bit but then I had to go to the bathroom.

I stumbled down the pier and made some friends. The smiles made me feel better but my body was aching. I was ready to go. Ninja caught two crabs and something big took his bait. I paced around for a while and finally told Sabre that my head was pounding and was running out of gas. He felt bad but I felt bad because if I wasn't hurting we could have spent the entire night out there. I just wanted pain relievers and some juice. It was hard to leave the oasis.

We stopped at the most crowded gas station in the world but they had what I needed. I focused on my breathing. Seven-seconds in, hold for seven and out for seven. I was told that will put you in a trance-like state after a while but my tricks weren't working. The migraine was alive.

I originally planned on stopping at the haunted Holiday Inn and La Quinta but was hurting too bad. By the time we reached Fountain, I was feeling alright. We stopped at a gas station and he grabbed some drinks. I remembered the story of the haunted lot across from Texaco. In the early morning, you can see a spectre for thirty-seconds. I wanted to report on it, even though it was night. We drove slowly, looking for the famous logo. We never found it. I think it was the gas station we stopped at. We will see next time...

We made it home and it felt good to climb up my porch. I greeted my cats and made some French bread pizza. I rolled up some of the good stuff only and took a glob of wax. I was feeling better but still a bit uneven. As we sat back and relaxed, I began to regulate. We laughed about Brigsley Bear and looked up videos about the Pensacola incident. We knew the kraken was near..

I was so drained of energy and basically fell asleep in the recliner. I remembered that I forgot my food tray on top of his truck and it still had my macaroni in it. Now I wonder where it fell off too. I wish Walmart had utensils, maybe that extra bit of food would have saved me from my headache. I later found out that those gummies caused other people pain. I was pretty sad about that.

That night, I had a crazy dream about a lake surrounded by a canyon. It was familiar but I don't think I have ever been there physically. I remember having to jump from a ledge on the edge and then windsurfing into a parachute. Everything was high speed and when I was in the water, I had anxiety. I woke up feeling slimy. I needed a shower. I know next time I see the coast, I'll be in better shape.

Recently, I heard a story down on the coast about cat people. Donnie from Standing Goats Rescue was partying near the Shrimp Factory back in the eighties. They would see a species of "cat people" lurking in the shadows. They were about three feet tall and had illuminated feline eyes. They were as fast as cars and ran on two legs. I believe they fed on the leftover shrimp waste and monitored the area. It is on my bucket list to see if I can find these beings!

CHAPTER 15
KAYAKING DOWN SPRING CREEK
JACKSON COUNTY, FL

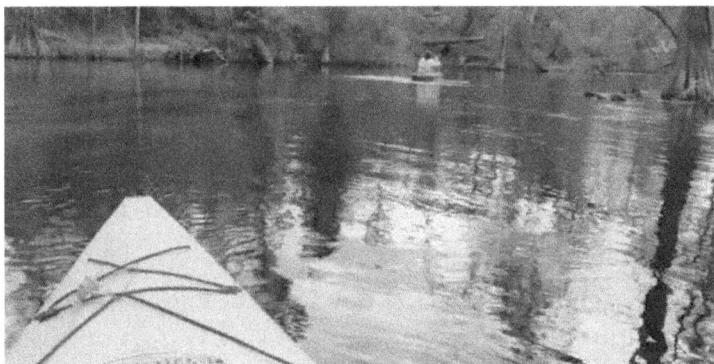

Kayaking with Ninja

'm laying down, writing this, enjoying the final opening day of Chief Wahoo. Grateful to be home in my warm cozy bed after a crazy freaking day yesterday. The day started with sunshine and clear skies but ended in a serious thunderstorm with pink lightning and strong winds. The gusts were ripping all night and are still pulling on my trailer today as we speak. My body aches but my heart still beats.

I started the morning with Godzilla vs Kong and some light meditation. I rolled myself a blizz and enjoyed the battle of the titans. There were tons of references to middle earth and colossal monsters. Pensacola was even attacked early in the movie. They had an Apex HQ that triggered the monster out of the gulf!! I really enjoyed the movie but I sure am ready for Zillafoot!

My phone rang and it was Sabretooth Captain, he saw our bigfoot bone news article and had a good laugh. He asked me if I wanted to look for the rest of the collarbone and of course I accepted. He told me to bring a life jacket and paddle. He would supply the rest. I packed up my gear and was out the door. I called my parents and sister to check in with my location.

I met Shinobi on Magnolia and parked my car. I hopped in his truck and we made a few stops. He traded in some games while I copped some delta 8 from the smoke shop. We picked up some snacks at the Mill Pond gas station. Every time I'm there, I recollect on the Cobragator destroying it in the movie years ago. I miss when it was Arrowhead.

We pulled across the creek into Spring Creek Park and loaded up the kayaks. We got equipped and hopped in the water. We wished good luck to some fishermen and went off to the jungle. The weather was great. I was enjoying the sun and getting my tan started for the summer. The water was clear and I could see the fish below my raft. There were tons of seashells and cool rocks. I imagined the amount of shark teeth and fossils below. I kept my eyes peeled for the megalodon or sabre-tooth pinnacle prize.

We passed Turner's Landing and went under the rail-road bridge. Woodpeckers were making sounds and we pointed out some daredevil squirrels. We saw many turtles, frogs and even one snake. I kept my eyes peeled for gators, crocs, and the skunk ape. It was paradise on the crystal water. We pulled up to the bend that ninja found the bone at but the water was so high, it was damn near impossible to find. We would be back.

We cruised on the river for a bit and then pulled off to the side at the next railroad. We searched for gems and I took some pictures. We finally were able to put a name to our graffiti ghost friend. Sabrecat said the name Tubby came from Final Fantasy but I figured it was just his street tag name. I burned one while I scanned through the rocks. I found a sick baseball sized obsidian with purple green rainbow colors inside.

We hit the creek and went upstream to a smaller meadow that we wanted to explore. We hopped off our yak and followed the branch for a while. We found some suspicious tracks and cool seashells. I took my shoes off and was walking in the sand. I kept my eyes peeled for water moccasins and territorial boar. I encountered some quick sand but it was good. We were looking for a hidden crystal spring but turned around after a while.

We were back on the water and cruising along. Captain found some fish traps and pulled them up to his raft. They were filled with giant crawdads. He freed the fish and looked for identification. It was his fish trap now. He just found one hundred dollars but more importantly saved the poor fishies. We finally made it to the big river and the water was much darker and deeper.

Sabercat knew of a dope spot up river a bit. He said it was a magical hidden spring filled with artifacts and gems. We kept to the edge and fought the tide. We searched for a good half mile and couldn't find the entrance to this hidden spot. The hurricane had rearranged everything along the bank. We finally turned around when it started getting dark. I thought it was peaceful until the dark skies turned to dark clouds.

We paddled fast as we watched the storm move in. My mind began racing. I was in water shoes and a short sleeve tee shirt. The plastic bag that had my phone in it had ripped. We were not prepared for a monsoon. I could survive some drizzle but the sky was turning red as pink strikes approached in the distance. It was pouring. Ninja yelled at me to slow down, adrenaline was just kicking in. I was terrified.

This is what David Paulides warns people about. Anything can happen in the woods. Nature will take unexpected turns and mother nature stays unpredictable.

We needed to stay close but I had to get the heck out of this wind and rain. I was mostly paddling with my eyes closed while the wind and rain stung my face. The lightning strikes were getting closer and ninja were yelling to keep our oars out of the water. Shock would have been instant death. I was not ready for hypothermia or pneumonia.

Our spooky visitor

After a while of blind paddling, I saw lights up ahead. I heard Stu yell that it was the highway. My mind was blank and my glasses were falling off. I couldn't tell if we went under the bridge or not. I asked how far and it was right ahead. We were fighting delirium and hustled toward cover. Finally we made it to the steep rocky edges. I barely made it while he struggled too.

We pulled up the rafts and tried to warm up. I was

shivering and could barely talk. I was attempting to dry off but was just so happy to be out of the rain. The wind was still whistling under the bridge. The cars rumbled the concrete above our heads but I was happy to be somewhat near civilization. We were still surrounded by forest but maybe could flag down a car in a worst case scenario.

Luckily, my phone was not broken. It was wet but I was still able to call my neighbor. Thank God he answered and just had gotten off of work. It was hard to hear him and even more challenging to describe where I was but he was on his way. It was monsoon conditions with sideways rain and intense winds. Pulling off on the side of the highway was going to be a high risk maneuver.

I hung up the phone and heard the ninja cussing. His raft had fallen in the water and he hopped in mine to track him down. I asked him if I should follow along but I couldn't hear him at that point. I waited under the bridge and called my home to update him. I kept peeking over my shoulder because now I was alone and this was the point of separation. Maybe something pushed the raft in...

I didn't know if Sabre would be back. Time was passing by quickly but it still felt like hours. I was freezing and also shaking in fear. I told myself to tighten up so predators wouldn't sense my vulnerability under this bridge. I was right along a hunting trail. It'd be an easy meal for a cougar or a bear. I was more scared of bigfoot or some feral people. The Creature from Black Lagoon wouldn't have surprised me at that point.

Modern day dinosaur

I called my neighbor and he was still about eight minutes from the highway. I actually told him to slow down to buy the ninja some more time. At that point, I was wondering if he had just taken both kayaks down the river to the next landing. I wasn't sure what was going on. I climbed up the steep incline to get a better look at the highway. Before the bridge was still the best location I could provide.

I dialed him up again and he was turning onto the highway. He put his hazards on and was asking if I could see him. I peered through the rain and saw a bunch of huge trucks beaming right towards me. They were probably surprised to see a dark figure rising up from under the bridge. The troll sightings before April Fools' Day were just wet old me.

I finally got a visual on his Honda Element and flagged him down. I crossed the highway and ran over to the car. I dropped my bag off and hopped in the back seat. I wondered what we should do. I considered going to the next landing to see if we could find him but I had to go down once more to see if I could find him. I ran back and down the steep hill, screaming his name.

After almost losing my voice and now soaked again, I heard him screaming from down the river. He was fighting the current and towing the other kayak. He barely had them tied together and was in rough shape. But he is a true warrior so nothing was going to break his spirit. I helped him pull the yaks up the steep ridge like we should have the first time and told him that our ride was up on the bridge. We stashed the gems and our yaks on the tree line. I left my snorkel and life jacket down there, I was just happy to be alive.

The ninja was plotting how to climb the tall fence on the left side of the highway but I had already seen that it was nearly impossible. I told him to follow me and climbed up the steep ridge. I peeked my head out and waited until there was a wide gap in the cars. I waved him on and we jumped the barriers and ran across the dashed lines. Double g let us in and we were so thankful.

We rode in the back of the Element as the wind pulled the car around on the highway. Cars were driving with their hazards on and the lightning strikes were blasting down. Trees were falling and small streams were forming in the ditches. We were lucky to be in the car. I had a lighter but I'm not sure if we would have been able to find enough dry stuff to burn. The wind was ripping too. It would have been hard to start. I would have maybe taken off my soaked clothes...

We pulled off the highway and I jokingly suggested going to explore the Dozier School. I stared into the windows as we drove by. We cruised through town and I pointed out the Russ House and other haunted mansions on the main street. The movie theater was bumping into the battle of the beasts. We passed Danny Lipford's pocket park and the hanging tree at the courthouse. Ninja told us he took sunset pictures the days before at the Elk's Lodge and soon enough we were back at the launch park. We thanked my homie and laughed about how we had helped him out in the past. What a beautiful cycle.

We hopped in the white truck and headed to my car across from Bear Paw. At this point, I was expecting it to be flooded out and my car to be washed away. Either that, or broken into. My mom's gear from the Hathaway Bridge trip was still laying across my empty passenger seat area. But all paranoia aside, the car was fine and we made it. I dapped up Sabre and told him to hit me up after he washed up.

I called my dad on the way home and he asked how

my kayaking trip went. I laughed and explained the rollercoaster ride experience. He was glad I made it safe and warned me to double check the weather, especially down here in Florida. I agreed and then told him that I had to focus on the roads. People were pulled off to the side, helping a tow truck or electrical company. I kept my eyes out for animals because this is when they'd be running wild.

I made it home safely and called my sister. I told her that I only made it to the bridge and she said I still probably had another hour on the river. I'm not sure how that would have gone. The rain was dropping horizontally and we could have very well been gator bait. There have been sightings of suspicious river dragons and other strange creatures in the waters as well. It would have gone really bad.

She was glad I made it and told me she would have picked me up if I hadn't found a ride. She told me to put my towel in the dryer and dress warm so I didn't get sick. We hung up and I hopped in the shower. I visualized how the day went. The warm sun on my face and the curiosity that almost killed us. The prints that we found have surely washed away. We worked so hard for all those moments. I remember wondering how the chapter would go midway through the journey. I could have never foreseen the climax. I know the conclusion has been written in stone long before last night but living it out, carving those memories, was exhausting.

At times I wondered if I had made my last mistake. I was prepared to call the cops if I couldn't find Sabre. I had listened to too many missing people's reports. I have heard the warnings about how crucial the first couple hours are when people go missing. I was worried about him. I was worried about us. I thought I was prepared and reality put me on my ass. I survived by the skin on my teeth but I might not be so lucky next time. I have to put more focus on my brainstorming before the missions. I need to be over equipped. And next time I'm wearing tennis shoes, I don't care if they get wet. I was practically barefoot out there. Madness. Lucky to be alive.

The ghost box was calling for Dana later that night. Not sure what that meant. I later returned home in my dreams. I always feel like I have somewhere to be while I sleep. It feels like I'm in the car driving around Brunswick and Bowling Green. Or I'm in the woods at my grandparents house. Recently, there has been a canyon. I do alot of swimming, flying and diving but I still don't know what's at the bottom.

Returned in June with the pirate ship to search for the precious stones. The Sunday waters were packed but I had a great time riling them up about the skunk ape. The rains came back and I was a bit scared. We burned one under an early bridge while the storm churned. We hopped back on the water and met a kayak fisherman who ran into three big gators earlier. That got my blood pumping!

We made it to the highway bridge and parked our yaks. We had a small picnic and then searched for the lost treasure. The grass was high and the snakes were near. Luckily we found a cool half submerged bridge that led to Terabithia. We followed a trail for about a mile until we reached the Final Fantasy spring. Truly magical. On our way back we heard a monkey sound from behind us. Very strange. It was multi-pitched. All four of us heard it.

No luck with the rainbow colored obsidian on this rerun but I know we will be back. Hopefully the gift I left for the pixies will be met with good fortune. They dictate what happens in that swamp so I want to stay on their good side. They've done a great job protecting and leading us so far! I told Cam about the sharks found in Dead Lakes! I hope that didn't scare him too bad!

CHAPTER 16
EXPLORING THE LETCHWORTH & VELDA MOUNDS
LEON COUNTY, FL

Letchworth Mound

The Lake Jackson Mounds might be the most well known prehistoric structure but it is not the largest! The Letchworth-Love Mounds date back to the Swift Creek and Weeden Island people and are the tallest in the state. There are about twenty-eight mounds in the area. Some artifacts excavated are nearly 12,000 years old! There are more than seven mounds that all face the same degree north in the immediate region. Talk about master architects!

The Velda Mound is hidden in the center of a residential neighborhood but holds some interesting legends. Neighbors have reported strange howls in the night coming from a glowing white wolf! Others have spotted a tribe of Native Americans conversing around a fire. They soon vanish in an instant when they realize they have been discovered. Both places were on my bucket list and magnetized my mind daily.

The day finally came to visit T Town and see what all this prehistoric fuss was all about. The Eta Aquarids meteor shower was later that night so the cosmic vibes would be aligned. If we were going to come across an anomaly or experience a miracle, it would fall on this block of the calendar.

I woke up and had a vampire podcast with Gypsy Road on his show Horror Talk. Sabre rolled over afterwards and we packed up. We had just bought some new tents and walkie talkies the day before. We had some drinks for Cinco de Mayo and talked about our Star Wars memories because the fourth was with us. It is always with us. We had to go to the source. That's how this trip was planned.

We hopped on I-10 east and went towards the Seminole campus. We passed the capital and hopped on 90. There were beautiful mansions and horse facilities blanketing the entire ride. The tunnel tree canopy was magical too. I felt like I was back in Ohio, riding through the Rocky River. Finally, we hung right and were on track to Letchworth!

We pulled into the parking lot and were the only ones there. I put three dollars in the pay box and went straight to the bathroom. I had to go bad and the same tactic worked at Lake Jackson! I did my business and then walked towards the first sign. Ninja was using the restrooms while I was waiting. Then suddenly I heard a smooth noise come from the forest. It sounded like the wind and air was being breathed out of the scrub.

It was hard to describe and not really alarming. It just proved to me that this place was here for a reason and so were we. Captain caught up and we followed the trail. There was a small mound on our left. We veered off towards the woods when we saw a small wooden structure. As we approached the wood line, we both heard a "Hawgh, hawgh" Not like a laugh, more like a grunt. Again it was strange but not threatening. No dread.

We moved slowly and scanned the forest but made it to the site. It looked like it was an old excavation structure. Sabre pointed it out and we later confirmed it from one of the park signs. We made it back to the pavilion and saw the pottery methods. There was a timeline of ancient structures across the world and this one was pretty respectable.

The Velda Mound

We moved towards the mound and my senses were tingling. This thing was massive! Not as tall as Kolomoki but it had a special feeling around it. The trees and overgrown bushes were a little messy but it showed Mother Earth will always reclaim. We circled the mound admiring the beauty, looking out for animals and orbs!

We took the Weeden Trail and came upon another Mound! I heard a strange sound in the bushes but we didn't get a visual. We hopped off the trail and checked out some uncharted territory. I found a couple tree bends. We circled back and heard the sound again. It was a snake but we couldn't find it! Then Ron pointed and I saw this beautiful beast. It looked like a eastern diamondback moccasin. I was thrilled.

It attacked our walking stick and we got some cool videos! We followed the trail and found some sweet berries! We picked the blue and black fruit and ate them on the spot. I scanned for the fae and tried to send positive frequencies through the region. We finished the trail and noticed a wildlife officer was hanging out in the parking lot.

We stuck to the trail and pulled back toward the mound. I took some photos and we made a video for my page. I admired the noisy forest on my walk back to the car. This was a magical place. I was glad to check it off of my bucket list. This is a must see in Tallahassee!

As we climbed in the truck, I noticed a tick climbing on my leg, I jerked and flicked it off of me. I shook out my hair and had Cat eyes check me. We found one latched on his leg. He sprayed it with some bug spray and left it on him. Strange method but I don't question it. The ranger probably had a good laugh watching us freaking out over bugs. Deadly insects!

We b-lined to the Velda Mound. We circled around the neighborhood arguing about parking before finally finding a spot near a house that looked empty. We explored the grounds and were enthralled! It's awesome that this serene spot sits right in the middle of the city. Even more strange that there is a glowing white wolf lurking around!

We didn't have any strange encounters but you could definitely feel the Native American presence. Someone was cooking a BBQ and I imagined the tribes catching and cooking a meal from the nearby creek. I appreciated my time there and tried to imprint it to my memory. The sacred soil will forever be with me.

Ancient days

After the Velda Mound, we stopped at Bass Pro Shop to check out the aquarium. We also were looking for snake boots and fishing supplies. It was cool but didn't touch the Highlands Cabela's near my grandparents farm. On the way home, we stopped at Ocheesee Landing. We scoped out the bank for fossils and I made a geocache video. I pointed towards where my mom and I found the sasquatch tracks at. It's under the flood now though.

Luckily, I got home just in time to get ready for my show with Beast TV! I was a little nervous because some of the community was upset with me over dropping some heavy knowledge on a show earlier in the week. They resorted to calling me a drug addict. They couldn't handle the truth so they attacked my beliefs, age and appearance. It had me rattled. Imagine someone arguing that the sky isn't blue. That's how I felt.

The show went great. Mark and Larry were open minded and had a ton of fun! Most of the community swallowed their words and realized their world had just been shaken. I compare it to a person who doesn't believe in sasquatch, having a scary encounter. Their entire past just melts. I believe that is what happened with a few of these people. Up is up and down is down. It's not too crazy.

I was wired for a couple hours after the show. My heart was still beating heavily and I felt like a huge weight had been lifted off of my shoulders. It's crazy I let it get to me that much but I'm only human. I enjoyed a couple dabs and swishers, listening to music and drawing. I turned on some Demon Slayer and remembered the special day in the sky.

At 1:40, I walked outside and was greeted by a beautiful "meteor" flying across the sky within the first five-seconds. I sat out there getting my eyes adjusted to the darkness. I fed the feral cats that live in the abandoned trailer and just soaked in the night. I didn't see any other meteors but the vibes were spectacular. I wondered if anyone else in the region was outside, grounding like me.

After a while, I went back inside and climbed into bed. I fell into a trance and became one with the sky. My trip was interrupted when I felt something crawling on me. My cats had fleas and I have long hair, so I'm familiar with the icky feeling of something on the surface of my skin but this felt worse. I was scared it was an entity but even more frightful when I discovered what it truly was. A tick!

I ran to the bathroom and flicked him into the toilet. I flushed it three times. Hated to waste the water but I did not need that sucker climbing back up into me! I wondered if he was on me the entire day from the mounds or just found me during the meteor shower. I went straight to the bath and got undressed. I was disgusted and even more scared. Were there more to me? Has the damage already been done? My body started aching thinking about it. I almost threw up.

I washed my hair twice and hopped out of the shower. I scanned my bed with a flashlight and even vacuumed the floor. Bed bugs, parasites and ticks just make my skin crawl. I finally climbed back into bed and reminisced on the magical night. I passed out shortly after with images of ancient temples and poisonous serpents on my mind!

CHAPTER 17
INFINITY CON AND BEYOND
FLORIDA STATE UNIVERSITY

Friend or foe (haunted pokemon)

nfinity Con was one of the best weekends of my life! I made a ton of new friends, took a lot of cool photos and found the inspiration I didn't know I was looking for. The convention was hosted at the most haunted campus in the state and the biggest live Super Smash Brothers tournament since the pandemic started, so you already know the vibes were right. I dreamt of this weekend for decades now, it was nice to finally walk it.

I closed at work on Friday and told the ninja I'd grab Mexican with him. I forgot that my neighbor was having a cookout so the dinner turned into beers. I downed two Victoria's and hustled out. I grabbed some last minute gear and went next door. We had steak and more drinks. I finished the night with a lit podcast with All Things Unexplained.

I tried watching the new Conjuring movie before bed but fell asleep about fifteen minutes into it. Woke up around three, two hours before my alarm. Had a headache from the drinks and of course started hearing noises in the other room. Next two hours rolled in sweat and sorrow.

I got out of bed at five and packed up the car. I had some time for peace and a dab. Drank some water and ate a banana to just get right. I was feeling good heading west toward Tallahassee. Nodded to Ocheesee Landing, famous ghost town and known cryptid convergence point. The highway was not just for cars.

Made it to the campus, admiring the architecture and overall vibe. Passed the White Witches Cemetery and sent my frequencies. Also nodded at the security of the Governor's Mansion! This campus has been stained by tragedy and mystery. The garnet and gold paint the bricks that hold this university together. Not even Ted

Bundy can break it down. The Wind still blows. We are deathless.

The Ghoul

I pulled up and saw the unloading station. I set up my table and explored the grounds. I ran into my neighbors in artist alley. Smash Bro pro Slampbell and Sci Fi Writer Bruce Ballister. He wrote a Panhandle tale about a guy finding an ancient relic under a fallen tree. Right up my alley! Slampbell is also an artist, I made sure to get a signed print of Spyro. I love dragons!

Soon after, Stephen O'Pry from Zombiearth showed up. I greeted him and soon after the doors were opened. Not long after, people were flooding the halls dressed in incredible costumes. I started off getting my grip and finding my feet. I remained myself and told them how I was the bigfoot guy and we have found bones, captured pictures and been run out of the woods by these creatures.

I sold a couple books but I was really making new friends. They loved hearing about the EMF detector and the dowsing rods. I had the replica of the Paddy footprint and their minds were always blown when I mentioned that she was a girl. And of course they wanted to know about Zillafoot!

Then a news team came over to my table and asked for some info! I talked to them about mound builders and the work that I have done. They loved my energy and said that I would be on Fox News Sunday night. Sadly I never got to see the footage but it sure was cool! Spread the word of giants!

Shinobi Captain showed up and was already the talk of the place within the first day. He stepped up to the axe throwing booth and continuously hit the bullseye target. Even the trained worker couldn't help but be impressed. Many people came up to us afterward thanking him for the show!

Bastille the Butler

We walked around the booths and admired all the creators. We met Roxy and Lemay from Star Wars! The rancor lived up to all my expectations! I even got to hold the bone! I got pictures with Bastille, The Butler, PikaBelleChu, and Fireteam Titan! Mike the Magician even made a card appear in my hand. Now that was cool!

The first day wrapped up and it was incredible! We stopped by the haunted Columns on the way home to make a video. I was drained of energy but adrenaline was kicking. When I got home, I chilled for a second then hopped on a three and a half hour interview with Dark Waters! One word...legendary!

Finally passed out and the alarm was ringing. I hustled westward and made it to the Capitol. I set up my booth quickly and then tried to round up some friends for a quick smoke session outside. I ended up solo dolo and timed it perfectly for the gates opening for the VIPs. The day started off slow but people started pouring in.

I continued to spread the word about our ancestors in the woods! I saw a couple familiar faces from umpiring and working at the game store. I posed for a couple pictures with people and even made videos telling their family members to be careful in the woods. The bigfoot booth buzz must have spread coz now people were coming to find me!

A former police officer came to my booth with an interesting story up in Bainbridge. His partner and him witnessed a goatman creature on Halloween morning. Another fella named Royce told me he had a photograph of the elusive beast. My buddy Kodi also told me about a famous photograph down in Lake Panasoffkee. I made sure to record them all! Like a true journalist!

My good friend Jack stopped by the booth! He was one of the directors of Zillafoot and makes horror movies himself! It was cool to show him the different makeup and visual fx people. I told him that he needs to have a table too! He laughed and said maybe next year. It was really nice of him to show up. To have some real life support, helps the ship sail smoother!

I also made sure to get some conversations with the other vendors. I recorded interviews with Bruce Ballister, Todd Kelley of Project Titan, Jay Magnum of Astral Genesis, and Josh Blackmon of Roller Derby Vampire Girl. I had to hear what real life phenomena may have inspired some of their awesome projects. I have major respect for any artist that has the cajones to market their product live and direct. We live in an age where the creators hide behind their work and there is a disconnect with the community. We busted that brigade! Live and direct!

My favorite booth was Ghoulash Games! There was a giant green ghoul named Goonther! I was lucky enough to survive the picture with the big guy. I sat down with the creators and got to hear the background story. I even got to trade my book for one of their games! I can't wait to play with the ninja one night. Let's see if we can get past the ghouls!

The panels and cosplay contest were lit but the Super Smash tournament was banging! It was sick seeing all the athletes competing! There cheers from the Top 8 were up there with a Florida State basketball game! It was good that in person live events are making a comeback. Down here in the Sunshine State, we've been doing this! Hopefully the rest of the world will follow!

After the wild weekend of Infinity Con, I was left

with many lasting memories. The rollercoaster ride of emotions is not for the weak hearted. You will reach some of your highest highs but you will also find yourself lost and confused for a lot of it. You just need to trust in your instincts and walk your own path. Your needs will be met in abundance when you are where you are supposed to be. Even when you smoke a joint in a restricted area, the picture is bigger than the sign!

CHAPTER 18
CHILDREN OF THE SON
POLK COUNTY, FL

Mid-Florida Research Team.

was super excited when I found out the Great Florida Bigfoot Conference was in Lakeland! It was at the Magic arena, just a couple minutes away from my old house. I knew this was my calling to revisit the grounds that truly created the Florida man vibe inside of me. I wanted to show my Panhandle Pirates the roots of what I experienced when I first became a Floridian but I also had some things to figure out for myself!

Tristin and Cam joined along for the adventure. They were incredible copilots on the road and important members of the research team in the woods. The brothers from Hidden Relief came prepared with MRE's, camping gear, and extra survival packs. They understood team-work and kept me calm when I got hot. It's all about balance. They took the trip to the next level!

We met at my place and went over the plan. Took a dab and hit the road. We stopped at Ocheesee Landing to pay tribute to the old oak and to get our eyes on Torreya. We knew sasquatch was over there so we tried to slow down and build the bridge. We wanted to bring some of that sacred energy over to central Florida.

We looked for fossils and burned a spliff. We peered across the Apalachicola and could feel the energy from the skunk ape central. It started to drizzle but was very peaceful. I found an awesome fossilized snail and this snake toy. I left the toy and kept the treasure as the guys showed me their finds. Then we were eastbound!

We filled up the tank near the Big Bend Jai Alai arena so we got some pictures. The drive was going smoothly until we hit some bad storms. The rain was pouring so hard that I was worried about the windshield. A Lot of cars pulled off to the side of the road but we kept pushing. Luckily we made it to 75 and had the Devil's Mill-hopper Geological Park on our sights.

We hoped the clouds would clear as we drove south. The storms came in spurts but we made it past Paynes Prairie and were approaching the entrance to hell. We were excited to see the legendary place that swallows up animals and spits out steam. We made it to the park and saw a bunch of caution signs.

We pushed onward and passed some other hikers. They told us that some of the stairs were closed and the trail was partially flooded. We didn't slow our stride and went right past the plastic tape. We climbed all the way down to the water and got a great look at the death trap sinkhole. I made a cool video and then we did the trail loop.

We kept our eyes out for signs of sasquatch but were really just happy to stretch our legs. There were a couple lizard sightings and tons of deer tracks but no monsters this time. We could definitely feel the presence of pixies. There were dragonflies and other buzzing beings in just about every direction. It was an amazing bucket list spot. Weird how the devil's den and devil's millhopper are in the same region. They probably connect above the aquifer.

Our next stop was the old Reddick High School! It was finally time to see the famous jail from Jeepers Creepers. Darryl and Trish tried to hide inside but this is where he broke in and killed the prisoners to regenerate!

We pulled up and it came to life. We circled the place enthralled by the magic. I was a bit nervous about my car being vandalized or the police bothering us but the mystery kept me gassed.

It felt like there were eyes in the windows watching us. The doors were bolted shut and there was a ton of graffiti. We finally made it to the famous door and steps. We took pictures as we visualized the movie scenes being made. A monumental horror movie and we were standing right where it was made. I've been to many locations and this was even surreal for me. I still remember getting the DVD for the first time. Thanks Josh... I still have Thirteen Ghosts too.

The crows gawked at us as we traced the perimeter. We tried to find a way inside but didn't want to get too crazy. We definitely plan on returning again. I'm sure they will tear the place down one day because it was pretty dangerous ruins. I want to explore the inside before that happens!

We were back on the road cruising in the Ocala area. I told them about the monkeys that got loose from the Jungle Cruise in Silver Springs and the orangutan lady that saved the camper with the broken leg. We got to Lake Panasoffkee and I mentioned the Unsolved Mysteries episode about the woman found by the hikers beside 75. Sad stuff but very interesting. We pulled off for one more detour and this was a big banger.

Jeepers Creepers jail

We cruised and did a U turn expecting to see an abandoned spot. There were cars and people in front. I told the bros that I'd go out there first and talk to them cuz they looked a bit intimidating. I walked out confidently and asked them if they could guess why I was there. They all replied "Jeepers Creepers" and I laughed. I introduced myself and they embraced us all.

We finally made it to the famous Diner. This is where Darry and Trish run to after their first encounter with the Creeper. They call the police as the monster pulls up and sniffs their clothing. Really spooky stuff and we were right there! The staff showed us a cool post card and BEATNGU license plate! We made a video and heard some more local bigfoot stories. Hope to be back Nov 6 for an event!

Finally we plugged Tim T's house into our GPS and I

was able to provide an ETA. We arrived around 9:30 and were greeted by a fierce guard dog Chloe at the door! Tim and Waynette had dinner and snacks all ready for us when we pulled up. The vibes felt like family reuniting and we knew we were exactly where we needed to be.

Originally our plan was to camp in the Green Swamp but Hurricane Elsa canceled all the sites. I was planning on guerilla camping on a dead end road or just posting up in the Publix parking lot for the weekend. But luckily Tim offered up his back den to us. That was a lifesaver. We met his other dog Baby and enjoyed laughs until about 2 am.

Cam and I stayed up until about 4 am just laughing and being delirious. We were drained from the journey but excited for the adventure. Finally I passed out and it felt like minutes later, we were getting up and ready for the big day.

It was an early morning and we were off to Lakeland. Bigfoot Dave came over to carpool and told us a story of how bigfoot lifted him in his tent. Crazy stuff. We hit the road and it all looked so familiar. It really kicked in when we hit 98 and I saw the places I used to visit. We were heading to Waffle House to meet more of the gang but I had a quick detour. I took a quick left and pulled into the Southgate Shopping Center!

The guys knew it right when they saw the arch. This is where they shot Edward Scissorhands and The Only and Only Ivan! This is where Johnny Depp cut hair and this is where the talking ape escaped! We took some pictures and admired the majestic structure. It took us back in time and then we were off!

We pulled into the breakfast lot and I was greeted by Matt from Central Florida Bigfoot. It was a blast and surreal meeting him in real life. I first met Tim while on his show and I'm thankful for the positive avalanche it has created. We chatted about our local ties and were all in a surreal moment! Then Florida Lonewolf and Marie Dumont rolled up and we went inside!

After breakfast, we all broke for the RF Funding Center. Well, they did, my car had a few stops to make! I took the brothers to Lake Hollingsworth and then rolled up through Florida Southern's campus. I told them The Waterboy was filmed here and the grounds were very haunted. I spent many days biking these trails and crossing these streets.

One time a guy tried to open the door of the car up front of us at a stop sign. Luckily they sped off. But then he tried doing the same thing to our car. That is until he saw what was pointed right at him out the window. We saw it coming from a mile away. He ran off like a cat caught in the dumpster.

We pulled up to the Annie Pfeiffer Chapel and I asked the guys if they ever heard of Frank Lloyd Wright. I told them he designed that famous Falling Water mansion. He was famous for using the golden ratio and I believe there is more to his work. I used to hang out by his statue when I just needed to get away! But when I wanted to see his ghost, I just visited the church. He is still spotted there to this day.

I told the guys we had one more stop. This was my big one. It was where I became a Floridian. Where some of my wildest dreams came true. I always wanted to work at the pub and live above the pub. Well, I got to join the musical and live with the band. I was living out of my car and luckily met the crew through couchsurfing.

We played punk rock shows all around the state and did a lot of spiritual research. I got to be in a feature length film and in many theatre productions. The house was truly a magical place, a sanctuary. We rehearsed the show there, meditated and smashed things in a glass corner. It was a safe place for people to get away.

It was nice coming back. I made a video about the shape-shifting neighbor and my old friend Larry Big Prine. I miss our walks and talks. Rest in Peace my friend. I'm trying my best to live the huna way. What are the odds a big Manson guy like myself moves next to a guy that stayed at Paul Crocketts ranch! Coincidence is the only thing to never exist!

Okay so we finally made it to the conference and of course smoked a blunt in the parking lot before going in. We met Flatrock Booger and talked to him outside with another researcher. We shared stories and photos. He has some incredible footage from his home surveillance tapes. The creatures in his woods come right up to his house!

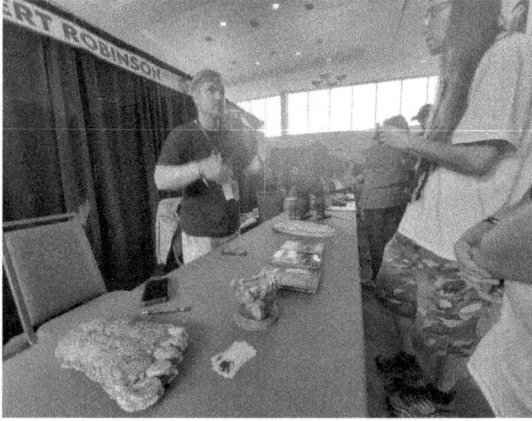

Robert Robinson

Then I spotted another cryptid approaching quickly! It was the Mogollon Monster! I was on his show and it started out great and went haywire! One of my most memorable shows but it left my heart pumping. We got into a flat earth debate and about a hundred people in his chat were running wild. I was a bit nervous about meeting him but we hit it off and ended up going on an expedition later that night. Mogs is the Man!

We got inside and I was in Heaven! Quickly ran into Rick from IKNOWSQUATCH! Then cdsquatcher and a bunch of other friendly faces. We went toward the stage and the show was ready to begin. Robert Robinson and

Dave Sidoti did a great job leading things off but I came all this way to see Stacy Brown!

Stacy is a Pirate, an Outkast and a brother! It was awesome to finally meet in person and talk about some of the local lore. We of course had to talk about Torreya and he gave me some incredible inside info! I told him a few new insights into the Ocheesee Pond Wildman case and wished him good luck on his speech. I knew he would kill it.

His segment was monumental and then it was time for the heavy hitters. The guys everyone came to meet and hear. Cliff and Bobo from Finding Bigfoot! We were lucky enough to meet Cliff and chop it up about Oregon and the mountain range. I told him about our mutual friend Tyler and how he lives on Mt Hood. Crazy brave.

Cliff had great history on the sasquatch people and Bobo provided tons of mind boggling audio from these creatures. It was cool to learn from the best and to see that we had many parallels. It was also super dope to hear Bobo's powerful bigfoot call. It dang near shook the arena!

Before I left I did a bunch of interviews! I chopped it up with the YouTube squad, a few authors and a doctor that brought a bag of apples that bigfoot tore open. That was pretty cool to hear. He is a very credible source and the full interview is on my channels. I suggest knowers, believers, critics to check it out.

We all gathered in the parking lot and planned out the night hike. Tim had the spot and now it was time to roll out. We stopped for food and gas, then finally arrived at the target. We crossed the train tracks and walked a dirt path along the wood line. We arrived at a flooded part and climbed back on the tracks. I was having flashbacks of Crystal Frog Cavern. My back pain was returning too but I continued on silently stepping on the wood.

The sky looked like the Fourth of July with the lightning fireworks. I was enjoying the show but some of the group began to grow weary. We pushed on, Tim had his night vision camera and Mogollon had a chest mount go pro. I was recording the audio but knew it was muffled because of the rocks sliding. I found a place we could dip back down into the woods but the storm got much worse. They sadly decided to go back..

We took our time on the way down the tracks, listening to the woods on the right and the swamp on the right. We burned one and hoped the smell would attract some energy. Zeus moved in and I'm sure the titans in the forest were active. We made it back to the cars and said our goodbyes. Then followed Tim home in a monsoon type front.

Luckily we made it to the haven and unwound. We were sad our nocturnal experiment got cut short but were super excited to check out the same location in the morning. Cam and I stayed up late, hanging out on the porch, mirroring the neighbors. They were having a great time too.

When we laid down for bed, the vibes were strange in the back den. All the boar heads staring and the bobcat on the prowl create an atmosphere. Tristin started wigging out while sleeping and it was truly strange. It lasted 3 seconds but I had to put my glasses back on to see what all the fuss was about. We were talking about falling so maybe we triggered him.

We fell asleep and got four hours instead of two! The morning came quickly but we were excited for the rendezvous. We were sad to say bye to Baby and Chloe but we promised we would be back. We made it to the grid and set up our equipment. I gave my go pro to Cam and made sure I had two bottles of water. It was hot and muggy.

We started into the woods and found some mysterious structures within the first half hour. We found circular tree bends that resembled portals and also many leaners. I discovered a couple ground glyphs and knew we were on the trace. We got split up and the red women found a track. Not long after we linked again, Tim discovered another! It was right next to some torn hunters' ribbons. Sadly it was too wet to make a cast.

We trekked on and found more anomalies. Then bang, the woman in green was running and flailing her arms. She had walked on top of an underground hornets nest and they were attacking her. I backed up and circled around and helped get them out of her hair. She was stung over 30 times and had to be rushed out of there. During the madness, Tim and Cam both recorded a strange baby cry on audio. No one seemed to notice in real time.

We pushed forward with heightened senses. We hoped the best for the two women. We came upon a group of owls. I call them a tribe because many Natives believed the fallen family was reincarnated as owls. I have heard many missing people and fairy stories associated with them so I take it as a telltale sign that something strange is near.

Not soon after, we found a hawk with a broken neck. The face was also a bit swollen. That definitely raised some eyebrows. We followed a nature trail and found a palm tree ripped to shreds up to about 20 feet. We theorized that the creature could have been digging for grubs or getting weaving material for bedding.

Then Marie Dumont found a deep track about twenty-five yards from the tree. Tim found another. It was a 54 inch stride. While we were examining the ground, we heard an owl call that sounded like it came from a man. It was one long loud hoot that came in one syllable. All the others were broken into parts. This got all of our attention and we had it recorded! Lonewolf went after the sound and actually got growled at through the brush! Scary warning!

The rest of the hike back was just trying to survive. I

was getting delirious from the heat exhaustion and dehydration. The bugs were eating me alive and my clothes were soaked in sweat. I had the chills but I knew I could just focus on my breathing and get by. We made it to the railroad and found many relics on the way back. Tim also mentioned he heard them whistling from across the tracks. We paid attention on both sides and T examined the barbed wire for more hair.

We made it back to the car and the trip was winding down. What a magical time. We were all worn out and ready for a nap but truly cherished all the memories made. Everyone made it feel like a family. I know there's a link between the Turner Farm and the Turner's in Winter Haven. We can't wait until next time.

Then we had our long haul back across the state. We filled up gas and I puked in the grass. That actually made me feel better. Traffic sucked but we made it back to the Central Time Zone. We stopped at the Ocheesee Landing to get our eyes back on Torreya and give our thanks. We found more fossils and that same snake toy! What are the odds! Magical! Great trip with my buccaneer brothas! Plunder till a hundred!

CHAPTER 19
FINITO

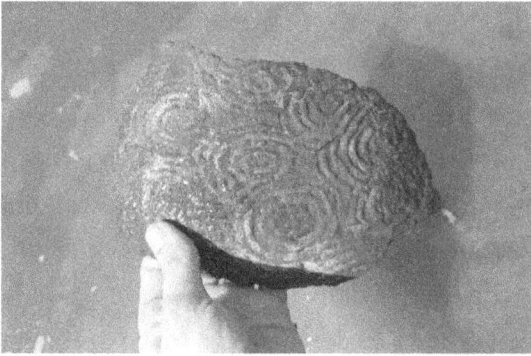

Ancient pottery

As we conclude this chapter of our adventure, we are left with many experiences and lessons to reflect on. We have found fossil evidence of creatures that are said to not exist. We have captured suspicious faces on multiple occasions in photos. Our team charted American pyramids and picked gold from the river. We have been intimidated by forces that are beyond measure and that still never slowed us down. We stayed focused when the water got rough. We stuck to our senses.

Where did it get us? What have we proved? What's the point of all this? These are questions that we are belted with everyday on our path. The ones who scorn and underestimate us are the same people who don't think we screen ourselves tenfold. They sit up on their pedestal and cast their shade. I'm not sure if they are familiar with dark rooms but it doesn't take a big spark to illuminate the entire chamber.

We do it for the memories. We do it for the adrenaline. The danger that presents itself in search of enlightenment has to be measured in a split second. Each breath may be our last. The power of the step is beyond our furthest thought. We do it for the conversations. The people we meet when we least expect it and most need it. We do it to live. We do it to learn.

We have been lucky enough to be interviewed by some paranormal experts to talk about our theories and findings. We have been on the news and even the front page of the paper! But the most rewarding part of our job is being invited out to people's houses and jobs to explore the paranormal. We have interviewed dozens of people and hopefully been able to provide an open ear and some closure.

In rare cases, the situation is too heavy for our pack.

We cannot stop the storms, we are not Dr. Frankenstein. We are what we are...treasure hunters that can sometimes match the frequency and vibration of supernatural anomalies. We have broken down the walls that bound most of society. We have entered realms that are low traffic. We use ancient techniques to reach the fourth kind but it's never just black and white.

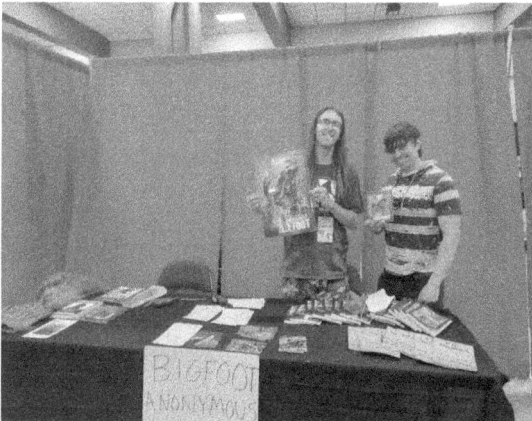

Altered Cortex Design

We are the messengers. We are a strand of the spiderweb. We are a thread of the red yarn that connects around all our ankles. We are you. We hope to be a reflection of your best qualities. Can only wish for you to pick up the good from what we provide and to learn from our mistakes. We absorb what is given and try to reciprocate it tenfold. We are the catalyst and so are you.

We urge others to dig into the stories of their family

tree and to ask the uncomfortable questions. The answers revived when the bubble of comfort are broken tend to be beyond philosophical measure. You cannot calculate the mind, body and soul when they work as a cohesive cycle. The blinders and blockers will attempt to intercept but the seeds of the truth will plant with the wind.

In life, we get attached to our shell but we need to treat our aura. We are protons and electrons vibrating at certain frequencies to create reality. We are all energy under the dome. The lightning strikes and shakes the firmament, creating thunder. The ceiling of heaven is closer than your favorite vacation location. We are particle form for most of our life but in true moments of being, we can become waveform.

If a dolphin and bat have echo locating and a lion has infrasound, then I believe our true ancestors had special abilities too. Octopus can camouflage while insects have flexible skeletons. We can use stones to breathe underwater but I'm sure mermaids have a better alternative. We believe we are on top of the animal kingdom, we are actually just a very small part of it.

The more we dig, the further we hike, and the less people we see, we notice certain trends. Trees bending certain ways, the predictable river and the alignment of berry bushes. There is a language in the forest that is always being whispered. Many people have no idea that geocache treasure hunts are going on right under their noises. Imagine if we knew what was going on right underneath our feet at this exact moment! Strange and unique has always been close to my heart. My mom's old work shared the building with a psychic. I was either peeking over there or fetching golf balls from the pond!

Spartans unite

The remnants of our past can help us decipher the future. The evil agenda has to announce itself through art and media. Predictive programming blinds the masses but nature has the answer. We have to break free from the matrix illusion and bound together. Our sacred energy can project us beyond the astral plane. We already have all the answers, we just need to unlock them. We need to find the right combination of frequencies to gain access to the hidden realm.

We will continue on our journey of adventure and

enlightenment but we need others like us. The good people of this world have been divided and conquered. We need to remind ourselves who we are. Hopefully our path will be guided by more angels than demons. The balance we yearn for is the simple catalyst that we need. A flower doesn't grow very well in a hurricane but the seeds will be spread. Find your map, it's out there! But more importantly, splice the mainbrace and make some memories!

CHAPTER 20
LETTERS FROM FAMILY AND FRIENDS

Tristin / Hidden Relief

This is the legend of the hog nosed bear around my home. My grandpa told me multiple encounters of a massive bear making its home in the woods around my house. My encounter I will share of said bear is when I was younger,

Tristin in Eden

my sister and I were kicking around a soccer ball in my yard around the tree line. We were having fun and enjoying the outside, it was a perfect day. We were interrupted by a loud roar that shook me, my sister confirmed that she heard it too by giving me a nod. I could tell she was just as scared as I was by whatever this creature was.

We made it to the house and decided to just assume it was a tree falling. The power behind the roar was too intense to be a tree. I know it's out there and to this day I still search for the hog nosed bear!

Our old house

———————

Cam / Hidden Relief

Jeepers Creepers diner

Me and T were heading back home down a road in Chipley till we got a feeling that something was watching us. We turn around and it was like half of a football field away from us but it look like it was crouched because we watched long enough for it to stand up like a big bear except it had yellow eyes. I took off leaving T after I said it was time to go he followed after then we suddenly appeared back at the house with our hearts pumping full of fear.

Sorry for the late reply. Was up late, T and I went to our lil cousin's birthday. The one who got chased by a six legged spider, fairy, pixie thingy!

Pre-historic arrowhead

———

Tim T in Florida

This Encounter happened in The Green Swamp West Wildlife Management Area in Central Florida. I was hunting in here in 1997 on a Special Wild Hog Hunt and right beside the Withlacoochee River, my hunting dog went into a very thick vine brush, there was fresh wild hog rooting everywhere. So apparently my dog got too close and messed up this being's hunt. There was a very loud sharp growl, it sounded like a Tiger, very powerful lungs, there was complete silence for several minutes. Back then nobody thought or talked about Bigfoot, I was thinking, what kind of animal out here can growl like that?

Well, after several minutes of complete silence and wondering if my dog was dead, here comes a wild boar hog running out of there with my dog running right behind it. The hog jumped into the river, my dog right behind it, my buddy's two dogs joined them with me and my buddy right behind them, we were all in the river, us, the hog and the three dogs. The hog made it to the bank on the other side, stopped beside a cypress tree with big cypress knees and fought the dogs for a minute. Then with the two of us still in the water the hog jumped over us and back into the river almost landing on my buddy, my buddy stuck the hog with his knife, the hog swam and circled us and went back to the bank.

He stopped to fight again giving us a chance to grab his back leg and kill him with my hunting knife. (This was a special Hog Hunt Only, my buddy's dad had the hunting permit and was the only one allowed to carry a gun, he was back up on the road at his truck waiting on us, we were his assistants on the hunting permit. My buddy's dad and a Game Warden that was on the road having a conversation, they both heard the growl and the silence. The Game Warden said, Well I guess your dog just got killed, and he left. There was no way they would have heard a growl from a bobcat or panther that far away. I have had a bobcat growl at me for a couple of minutes straight from about 15 feet away from me, it was nothing even close to the growl I heard that day.)

Tim T with wild boar hog

I believe it was around two hundred pounds. Wild and Mean. This was also shortly after I had returned home from military service in the US Army. Also shortly after this encounter I found a dead six point whitetail deer, in the same area another weekend on a Special Wild Hog Hunt. I found this deer because of my hunting dog wandering over to a creek and he was pulling at something. We walked over to him and there was this buck laying in the water with part of a log over it, hiding it. The deer was pretty freshly killed and this creek was to far inside the hunting area for a poacher to have traveled to kill and then carry a deer out of this Wildlife Management Area. I cut the Antlers off and brought them home.

Antlers

Winnie's (Waynette Turner's) Story of her encounter, Waynette was at home with her older sister and mother on the outskirts of Winter Haven, Florida. In Central Florida, Polk County. Around 1975 or 76. They lived beside an orange grove with more orange grove behind their house since their father worked for Jack Berry a major orange grove owner in Polk County at that time.

It was late, around 11pm at night, the three of them started feeling heavy vibrating footsteps outside the house, and it would follow them on the outside as they walked down the hallway. When they went back down the hallway it would follow them still going in the direction they went. Their mother got a shotgun and had it ready. They believe it went around by the back door, hit or tried the door knob which was locked. Then it had moved on away, they didn't hear it anymore after that.

Encounter location

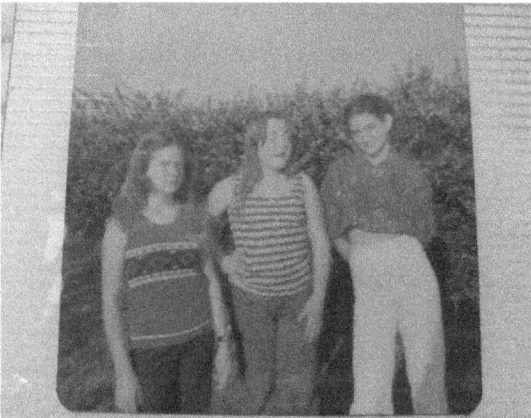

The sisters, L-R: Waynette and Kristal, unknown
third person.

One of Waynette's older brothers and his friend were driving the family car around in the orange grove beside the house, around that same week or so. The two boys were in their upper teens and driving the car for fun and entertainment around the orange grove. These orange trees beside their house were young trees about 6 foot tall. This being that they believe to be a Florida Skunk Ape, attacked the car from behind and was bouncing it up and down.

One of Waynette's other brothers saw the Skunk Ape's head above the trees, which would have made it at least seven foot tall. Waynette's brother, Wallace, that saw its head above the trees still remembers this incident as though it happened yesterday. This same brother has also told us that neighbors nearby also had incidents with this creature around the same time. And when asked, Waynette's sister confirmed the encounters just as Winnie remembers them.

––––––

Donnie from Standing Goats Rescue

If you go out to the Apalachicola forest at night you will see the balls....most are basketball size, white, yellow, blue, and pink. Other people have claimed to see many other colors, but I haven't seen but these. There's no noise from them at all, but the strange part is that some of them will make you feel really uneasy...almost like you're in danger. I don't remember if there was a specific color that caused that feeling or not...but I did experience it a few times. I always thought they seemed mechanical in a way, because almost all of them are in the same height above the ground. For years I assumed it was ball lightning, but now I believe it's some kind of life form or spirit form. I seen them only four or five times….while hunting. I would stay in the woods until it was dark, then I'd head to the boat. That's when I saw them. If any of them get close to you, there's a weird feeling you get that is similar to static electricity. …the hair on your arms and neck will stand up. That's the reason I thought it was ball lightning. I'm certain that the wildlife and insects can see them too because it gets extremely quiet when they come around. I don't know what they truly are, but they are very fascinating to see

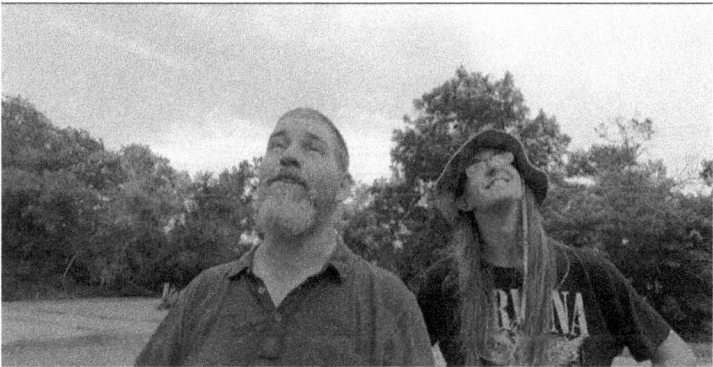

Donnie and me

I've had some of my family tell me and a couple friends a story about how they saw a goat man and tried to chase them and they said they didn't stop running but neither one of them will go to the train tracks down the road. Now the other day me and my friends Josh and Christon went down it at night and found a workers' vest that had blood on it but we got chased back down the tracks by something that wasn't human. a tree fell too but we all ran so fast out of there. but now they told me they won't go down there with me at night again but when you walk around madrid and down the tracks it doesn't matter it always feels like someone is watching you...

————

Bryan

Outside the conference. L-R: Matt, me and Mogs

It's been good on my mountain lately. The rain and snow kept me away this week. But last week. My 2 Bigfoot friends were sitting around the fire and there were 2 on each side. They kept mimicking back and forth a few times with weird bird noises. We just kinda let them do their thing and didn't walk over to them. I have the pathways all figured out. I think I might have seen legs walking early in the morning. Was a Bigfoot or a big box cat.

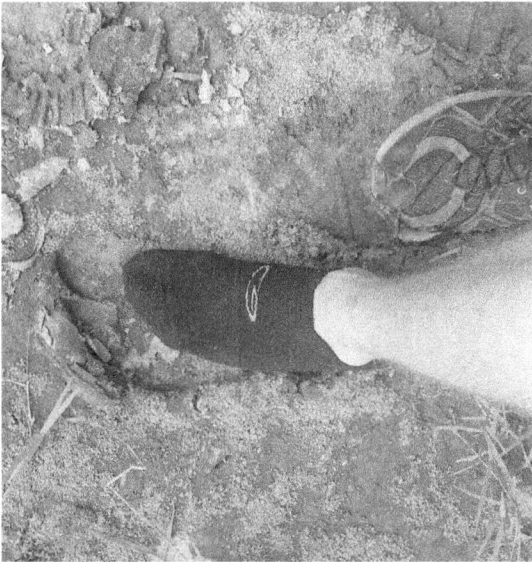

Giant footprint compared to mine

Weeks later... The mountain has been really good. We did some work with the tractor and we all woke up with the sound of an African lion waking us up behind tractor at 7 in the morning

Green Swamp Squatch

———

NE and Oak

I heard sasquatch screams just outside of Baxter last fall at a campground on the golden road, mile marker 25 from millinocket on the deadwater. I was with a party of 4 and we all heard it and agreed not to talk about it. I don't carry a gun because I know the sasquatch hates them, and I know they watch me a lot. I don't think a gun is saving anyone who is going missing either. It's either going to happen or it's not. I say a lot of prayers and make my intent known to whatever is out there I want to be left alone and am not there to bother them... seems to work although I did find fresh sasquatch tracks (huge ones) two days ago where we found that big moose antler in a peat bog. That was the first time I have found more than 1 track as well.

Outkast Paranormal

Cliff Barackman (from Finding Bigfoot), me,
Cam, Tristin and Mike

OGVril

Edward Scissorhands filming location

Wake up, I'm strapped down to a table, at my feet is either 5 or 7 beings, I don't know which, but I know it was an odd number. In the middle stood a tall draconian, and the others were shorter grey/draco hybrids. One moved to the right side of the bed and looked down at me, I started thrashing, extremely violently to the point I was bouncing on the table under the restraints, shouting repetitively "NO, NO, NO, NO". After a few seconds, one of the hybrids moves to the left of the table, brings a machine down from the ceiling, it looks like a gun with blades on the front, and places it on the inside of my left elbow, I black out.

I wake up in the middle of the night, thrashing around, screaming, soaked head to toe in sweat. During this time of my life (roughly August, 2019) I was lifeguarding, and while at work I was thinking about this, only believing that it was an odd, highly detailed, bad dream.

Green Swamp footprint

But then I looked down at the inside of my left elbow, where at first I noticed odd red marks, creating a Y with a horizontal mark in the intersection, more like a ¥. Between this horizontal line and the bottom mark, I noticed brand new, fresh scar tissue, blueish purple in coloration at first, ovular in shape.

For the next eight months, I would have nightmares

every time I tried to sleep, anywhere between 6-14 times every night, including whenever I tried to nap. The nightmares were just a replay of the abduction, replaying it back to me over and over and over again. I would wake up the same every time, thrashing, screaming, soaked in sweat. The scar and red marks healed completely within a few days, but I can still see a very slight different texture of my skin where the scar was.

Carving of a pirate ship

ABOUT THE AUTHOR

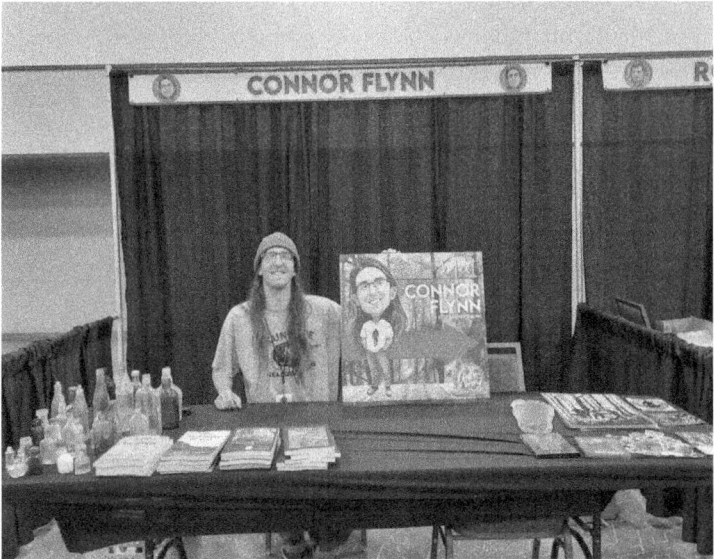

Connor Flynn is originally from the coast of Lake Erie and now resides in the Florida Panhandle. His love for outdoors and investigative journalism has led him down many paths of strange and unusual things. Flynn has appeared in films "Zillafoot" and "The Void Cat" and hosts a horror themed podcast. Catch Connor in the swamp or on the screen, he stays active in the field always waiting for a scream!

Visit him at his YouTube Channel below and on other social media platforms.

YouTube: https://www.youtube.com/channel/UCvcN_fkxz1wtjgwibEtF6qQ

ALSO BY CONNOR FLYNN

Erie Swamps: Road Trip to Eden

Big Brother, Bigfoot

Monsters & Mysteries Around the Corner